Back to One

A Practical Guide for Psychotherapists

By Sheldon Kopp

Science and Behavior Books, Inc.
Palo Alto, California 94306

Library of Congress Card Number 77-608269
ISBN 08314-0055-2

Contents

IMITATION—"In imitation there should be a tinge of the 'unlike'. For if imitation be pressed too far it impinges on reality and ceases to give an impression of rightness."*

Seami

Some fragments of BACK TO ONE originally appeared in *Voices*.

I am grateful for the competent and responsible editorial assistance of David Kopp.

Chapter 1

West Meets East

This may be the first of my writings that you have encountered. It is my seventh book. It is just another fragment, the most recent in a sequence of writings[1] that reflect my own development both as a writer and as a psychotherapist. BACK TO ONE is simply that work on my Self which it is time for me to do *now*. In undertaking the writing of this book, I found myself drawn to the question of how to present it in perspective for those readers who do not know my earlier work. My most conscious interest is in making sure that I do not thrust it at the reader out of context in a way that would mislead as to its place in his or her own work.

Though I choose the Oriental metaphor of Yoga for the Occidental practice of Psychotherapy, I am not of the East, but of the West. My wish is not to lose my Self, but to find my Self. I seek not the Attainment of Perfection, but the Acceptance of Imperfection.

My current immersion in the issue of self-discipline follows a period of exploration of abandonment and self-expression. The seeking of non-attachment follows an intense surrender to deep involvement. The seeking of the separation of my Self begins on the heels of years of being a close companion of other exiled pilgrims.

How then was I to set the scene, to point to the detachment of yoga within a background of deeply felt human contact? As it turned out (as it always turns out), the answer was being prepared even before the question had yet been formulated.

Months before I knew that I was to write this book, I received the kind of letter to which I usually do *not* reply. A Graduate student named Judith Schmidt at the California School of Professional Psychology was doing her doctoral dissertation on personal approaches to psychotherapy, on "Psychotherapy as Paths of Being." She wrote to ask me (among others) to answer a set of questions which would reflect how I came to do the work I did.

1

This time I did choose to respond. Without hesitation, I sat down at my tape recorder and dictated my responses to her "interview." Months later, as I began to write this chapter in a book not yet conceived at the time of the interview, I received in the mail a copy of Dr. Schmidt's dissertation.[2] It was then that I first knew that the Forces of Darkness had once again conspired to present me with just what I needed just when I needed it. Intriguingly, again I myself had been the unknowing instrument of my fate, with Karma again turning act into consequence. Again inadvertently I accrue the powers I need to tempt me at this point on my trip. Again I will let them be used without concern for the results of my efforts. Again I will witness their Work and merely attempt to move on.

But for now, share with me the unedited fruits of my Siddhi.

Q: For how long have you been a practicing psychotherapist?

R: I began in 1951.

Q: What made you want to become a psychotherapist?

R: When I was fifteen, in the midst of a great deal of adolescent sexual turmoil, I read *Psychopathia Sexualis* by Kraft-Ebbing. His descriptions of all the perverse activities which I had been living out in my masturbatory fantasies, led me to decide immediately to become a psychiatrist and to save all these poor souls. Also, of course, I wanted to cure my crazy family. More thoughtful and compassionate motives developed later. I guess it was like going to an art museum at first for the prestige of it, but coming back because of the powerful impact of seeing the paintings.

Q: What has your professional training been?

R: I was an undergraduate in psychology at New York University. I took clinical training in psychology at Brooklyn College, mainly at King's County Hospital. I completed my Ph.D. at the New School for Social Research. I got lots of random supervision here and there from people for whom and with whom I worked. I had several personal experiences as a patient in psychotherapy. I attended encounter groups, workshops, and training seminars here and there. I was, of course, best instructed by my patients.

Q: What made you select this training?

R: I didn't know any better. Much of my schooling was

irrelevant and in some cases destructive to my ambitions to be a psychotherapist. Mostly I flew by the seat of my pants. I might have been a lot better if I had known someone early in my work who could have guided me.

Q: What was your early vision of the ideal experience of what it means to be a psychotherapist?

R: I suppose that there were many metaphors for what I hoped to reach. I was to be a guardian angel. There was, of course, also my Moses trip. Leading the children of Israel. But I became sick and tired of only going to the mountain top myself. And there was a strong wish to travel into the depths, the darkness of the soul.

I was uncomfortable with what I grew up to think of as normal people, and sought extremes, peculiar people, oddballs, street types, criminals, near-criminals and aspiring criminals. I felt so painfully peculiar myself that I think I was looking for a community of exiles which I could join.

Q: Did you have any early inspirational models upon whom you patterned yourself as a therapist?

R: Yes, I suppose so, but they weren't therapists. Who were they? Oh, people like Baudelaire, Verlaine and Rimbaud. People who had made the dark journey into the pit of their own souls. I remember one essay being very important to me when I was quite young. It was Simone de Beauvoir's piece, "Must We Burn Sade?", in which she made out a case for how helpful the Marquis de Sade was simply because he disturbed us with his writings by insisting that *everything is permitted.*

Q: Can you please share something of the course of your self-growth since your early training and practice as a psycho-therapist?

R: I think that I went from being someone who was first a semi-delinquent, sensation-seeking existential adventurist, to some sort of righteous, arrogantly-presumptuous, stuffy character who thought that he knew everything. Then into some kind of immersion in mock-humility during the time when I was going to become a simple saint.

And now some conglomerate of all of those things. With enough of my share of pain so that I've become a fairly decent, giving human being, less embarrassed by my own mistakes and more interested in what I am doing than in its results.

Q: Please describe some of the pivotal experiences and decisive events as they relate to the preceding two questions.

R: I'm going to interpret that question very narrowly just to make it easier for myself. At twenty-one I went into individual psychotherapy twice a week for two or two and a half years as a way of trying to break with my family and get my shit together. A few years later when I was about ready to do my dissertation, I became paralyzed. I seemed to refuse to go on or couldn't go on to get the Ph.D. because it felt like giving in to the demands of people around me. At that point, I went into group therapy for a couple of years. Got free of my stubborn insistence that I wouldn't give in and surrendered to accomplishment.

Several years ago I developed a brain tumor. Went through a series of operations. Got very, very strung out with a lot of old, old pain. Tried to push past it, finally crashed. One summer, I was going to kill myself. Got through that awful time and back into therapy once more. This time more as a matter of kind of moving toward some sort of self-acceptance than toward any particular growth. I don't mean to minimize; it saved my life.

Of course, the pivotal experiences of my marriage, my relationship with my wife, my kids being born and growing up, my friends, my enemies, all kinds of other things played their part. But I will resist the temptation to give you an autobiography at this point.

Q: What transformations in yourself, if any, do you presently hope for?

R: Nothing too specific. But I guess I can say a few things. I want to become more self-accepting, to have more joy, to live with things as they come, to be more tolerant and less blaming of myself for the mistakes and foolishness that have to come every day. I'd like to live with my physical and emotional pain with more grace. To treat the people that I care about with more benign indifference. That is, to be with them without asking that they be something other than they are. I want to stay alive and alert to my feelings. To feel things more deeply. To enjoy my excitement.

It's hard to be more specific. I'm not in that kind of space at the moment.

Q: Are there any activities that you're involved towards such actualization?

R: I suppose the concrete things are my writing which always instructs me. Some non-ritualistic meditation. And, of course, doing therapy, which is like staying in therapy the rest of my life.

Q: Has your own growth altered your theories regarding your image of what a whole self-actualized fully-functioning person is? What makes a person less than the above? How does a person change in therapy? Please describe the nature of such theoretical changes.

R: I'm sure that my own growth has altered my theories. I don't think of my approach as theoretical, but it must be, from a certain point of view. I think that the changes I've gone through make clear to me that all people are as weak and as strong as anyone. Everybody is vulnerable. Everybody makes mistakes, everyone fucks up. They have delightful parts of them, things to be enjoyed by them and about them. I suppose it has to do with moving toward expecting the unexpected, accepting the imperfect, trying to understand people as being responsible for their lives without being to blame for them.

Self-actualization can only come after people break out of some of the reductive, risk-avoiding, safe, familiar patterns by which they stereotype their lives. In therapy, part of what I would try to provide is a safe, nurturant atmosphere in which the patient and I get to know each other, in which I reveal my own frailties and strengths as an invitation for them to reveal theirs. I only take on patients whom I like up-front, as they are, so that there's no requirement on my part that they change.

Q: How, if at all, have you changed in terms of how you view the nature of the relationship between yourself and the person who sits across from you in therapy?

R: I think at worst my original notion was that the person was some kind of specimen whom I was to be curious about. Some sort of case to be cured. Now, it is someone whom I will allow to become important to me, to whom I will be vulnerable.

Clearly, now, I feel that it's an accident that I'm the therapist and the person across from me is the patient. It could easily be the other way around. And sometimes is.

Q: Does this reflect any change between your former and present views regarding the nature of the therapist-patient relationship? Please describe the nature of any such changes.

R: I still see myself as the expert. That is, in terms of having a commitment to do my own trained disciplined best, to be useful to the patient, to help him or her to be happier. But, I'm not the authority and they have to define their own happiness. I run the therapy. They run their lives. I work with the patient and come to care about the patient, but I really don't care what the patient does.

What he or she does in terms of changing in therapy is not an index of whether I'm doing my job right or not. My attention is on doing "impeccable" work, in the Castaneda sense of the word, the Don Juan sense of being the impeccable warrior. Sometimes when I do things very very well, the patient doesn't change at all. Other times I might be doing a half-assed job and the patient, because of being in very good space, picks up whatever I'm into, adds a great deal of his or her own stuff and makes excellent progress, from his or her point of view. I find that to do the best work, I have to free myself from anxiety about the results. A kind of Karma Yoga position, I guess. So the change is partly more respect for the patient, less arrogance about myself and more detachment about what's going on.

Q: Have there been any specific people who have influenced these changes? Please describe the nature of such influence.

R: Since you ask for specific people, I think I'll interpret this question quite arbitrarily, in terms of people whose work or writings have been of particular influence in my own work. Sometimes they've been people I have known and spent time with. Sometimes they're people with whom my only contact has been reading or listening to their words. They'll be in the order in which they come to mind. This does not suggest any priorities except at an unconscious associational level. The therapists who most influenced me are Carl Whitaker because he's so comfortable with his craziness; Carl Rogers because he's such a decent, uninterfering sort of guy; Fritz Perls because, although he was a smart-ass, he was a brilliant magician; Carl Jung because, despite all his murkiness, he helped me get more deeply into my own powers. Some of the other people who have influenced me are Martin Buber, the Baal Shem Tov, the Zen masters, Baba Ram Dass, Lao Tzu, Camus, Erv Goffman, Erv Polster, Joen Fagan, Don Lathrop, Dylan Thomas. The above were not all professional therapists, of course, but they each gave me a clearer sense of ways of touching meaning and touching other people. Bessie Smith put me more in touch with a certain kind of earthiness. There are others in jazz and blues who have done that as well. Faulkner taught elaborateness; Hemingway, simplicity; T. S. Eliot, elegance. That's all that comes to mind at the moment.

Q: Have the kinds of persons you preferred to work with changed over the years? And how?

R: Yes. I think that earlier on, because of my own willfulness, I was more interested in working with patients who seemed irresponsible to me—psychopaths, and certain other kinds of character disorders. Now I prefer to work with people who are harder on themselves. Neurotics, whom I would help to be more self-accepting. I suppose, too, that in the earlier work, I tended to choose the hardest patients—schizophrenics, psychopaths. Now I choose the easiest patients.

Q: Has there been any single session or series of sessions that you as a therapist have experienced as critically illuminating with regard to what you hold as the deepest meaning of therapy? Please describe.

R: That question seems too hard to me. If I get the answer to that question together, I'll probably produce another book. To answer it in no less a cavalier manner: Yes, there has been a whole kaleidoscope of such experiences, some of which I have described in my writings in which patients have illuminated my work and, indeed, even transformed my life.

Q: What are the ingredients present in those therapeutic transactions in which you experience yourself as being most alive?

R: I suppose they're the ones in which I'm doing the most improvisation and the patient is presenting the most surprises. Now I get a lot of good feeling out of doing excellent work, understanding fully much of what's going on, seeing something come up out of a particular adaptive context, seeing the derivative material with a patient, knowing when to make an intervention and of what sort, and of doing the work so well that the whole session, or series of sessions, becomes a kind of centered, integrated experience.

But, as to being most alive, those are riskier times when new things come up which I had either never considered or never run into or at least never thought of in the ways in which they're coming up. In which I get thrown, make mistakes, fall down, get up. In which the patient helps me as much as I help the patient.

Q: What, if any, changes have evolved in what you consider to be the essential goals of psychotherapy?

R: I think earlier on I was probably more involved in problem-solving therapy, in which I was helping people to work out the answers to a particular problem or to "cure" certain disorders that they were into. Now I think that I'm much more a growth therapist. It's very open-ended. First of all, I accept the patient as being in an okay space except for the ways the patient defines as unsatisfactory. And also I'm willing to make the trip beyond the problems. You don't have to have problems to be in therapy with me. In fact, I always thought that I'd like to be in the position where I saw only patients who had already been cured by other therapists. And I guess I like to get the patient curious about what his or her life is about, where he or she might go, how to become who he or she is.

Q: Do these changes in your views manifest themselves concretely in your therapy work and how?

R: Yes, I'm sure they do. In terms of my being much more accepting of the patient, of having confidence that the symptoms or problems will be resolved. I will tell the patient: "That's a solvable problem. We'll get it worked out if we get to know each other enough. If we spend time in good space together, the problems will be solved." Not that occasionally I won't do *some* problem-solving work. But in the main I feel like most emotional problems are problems of *attention*. So that if you get the patient unhooked from that stuck place by increasing awareness, then new things can be done. I guess partly what I do is fuck up his or her trip through my therapist tricks so that usual ways of behaving don't work anymore. Then, in the midst of that confusion, the patient comes up with other ways of doing things. And we get to new spaces.

Q: What are your views as to what you as a therapist should and should not disclose of yourself to your patients?

R: That changes some. But I guess I reveal a great deal of myself. I tell my story as the patient tells his or hers. I reveal my childhood. I reveal the problems that still go on with me. I reveal some of the delightful things about me and my life. I reveal my feelings about the patient. I suppose the limitations are in part that I won't reveal something that I'm so much in a struggle with that it would burden the patient. Or, if I'm too scared. Because if my anxieties are too high, I'm not going to be able to do the work.

There are, of course, times when I would set aside my need to disclose myself because it doesn't seem to be in the patient's best interest at that moment. And I'm also sure that I get into the human trap of sometimes presenting myself as better and sometimes worse than I am. For the most part, though, I think that the patient has to get to know me if he or she is to be able to trust me at all. And I have to make myself vulnerable and reveal myself if I'm going to be able to trust the patient enough to be helpful.

Q: Are there any facets of yourself which you think are crucial to disclose to your patient?

R: Well, up-front, I feel that I have to deal with the issue of the fact that I don't have long to live. That I have this brain tumor. That I have a lot of pain. That if the patient gets hooked up with me, then probably I'm going to become important, the patient is going to have to go through some of the pain that people who care about me have to endure. I warn a patient of this before we begin. It would be unfair to take one on otherwise. I also will let the patient know about my biases and my particular styles so that he or she doesn't feel crazy when running into my need to show off, my fascination with evil, my need for closeness and warmth—stuff like that.

Q: Have your attitudes toward these two questions changed over the years? How and why?

R: Yes, of course, they have changed over time. At first I used to try not to disclose anything, so I disclosed my fearfulness. Then I got into disclosing just the good things about me—problems that I had already solved. And in that way, I unwittingly disclosed my righteousness and my presumptuousness. I think that some of the reasons that I've changed about this is that some patients have been so responsive, so kind, so decent, so much more generous with me than I am with myself, that it's made it much easier to show more and more of myself.

Q: Are there any parts of yourself that you will not disclose to any patient? Why not?

R: Yes, of course there are things that at a given point I may feel ashamed of or that I may rationalize as not useful or as damaging to the patient. I'd be into some number of my own of hiding myself. The other thing I think is that sometimes I will not reveal some aspect of myself, partly because it would mean betraying a confidence of someone else close to me. I will tell stories about where I am, partly in terms of where I am with my wife, or my kids, or my friends or, anonymously, with other patients. But sometimes that puts the other characters in the story in too bad a spot and so at some points I will draw the line on that.

I think I'm trying to work on this in that my present writing project is a collection of papers to which I've been inviting people to contribute. It's called THE NAKED THERAPIST and the idea is to get myself and a number of other well-known psychotherapists to reveal times in which they made mistakes, or were embarrassed or ashamed when they were with patients. As a way of showing more about how to deal with those feelings or, more correctly, so that I can discover in writing this book more about how I might deal with those feelings. This is an issue in which my answer might be coming across in a contradictory or confusing way because I'm very much in process with it.

Q: Do you recall any time in which you would have liked to disclose some aspect of your life to a patient but had difficulty in doing so? Could you please share this experience?

R: What comes to mind is the experience of a few years ago when I was so incredibly depressed and also pretty actively paranoid after the first operation. I think I just felt too awful to show patients where I was, especially early on in a time when I went back into therapy. Because one of the things I was feeling was: if I feel so bad and so hopeless, then who the hell am I to try to help somebody else? It's interesting, because later on when I felt in a better space and revealed to patients just how down I had been and how crazy I was, in a couple of groups, the patients said to me, "Oh, we knew that you were crazy and figured that you were struggling, but you did a pretty good job anyway." They were just delightful. I cried.

Q: What do you see as central to the training of future psychotherapists?

R: I feel that the main thing is that psychotherapy is a folk art. Most of the scientific training is garbage. I don't think that it's useful at all. I think of the formalism of graduate schools, except for a few recent experiments, perhaps the California School, maybe Humanistic Psychology Institute and a couple of other places.

But most of this stuff is really an emphasis on thinking, away from feeling, away from intuition, away from meeting immediate experience.

It takes years to get out from under all that crap.

I think that psychiatrists are treated to a program of education which suggests that the patients are cases and should be dealt with in that way—as if they have medical problems, the whole doctor-patient number. Psychologists are given a conceptual business in which they get a kind of *negative* detachment, thinking in terms of scientific constructs, in terms of subjects rather than people. Social workers are often trained to be super-benevolent, enabling speakers for the voiceless, kind of grand dames out of the lady-bountiful syndrome. The ministers are given some sort of Christ-like role. All of our training is not only useless, it's damaging.

I feel that the best training might be in small experiential groups with a therapist apprenticing with one and then another seasoned therapist as supervisor or guru, with a lot of work with patients.

It's crucial as far as I'm concerned that therapists have therapy themselves; that they not be emotional virgins. That they've tasted some of the pain of life and dealt with their own struggles. It's the only thing that gives you a decent respect for the people who come to you for help.

Q: How do your views here relate to your present day assessment of your own professional training experiences?

R: I think that my professional training experiences were mainly poor and irrelevant. I got lucky a few times. A lot of what I got came out of being a member of the American Academy of Psychotherapists which was, at that point, a maverick group of some very talented people who were interested in sharing a great deal. But, for the most part, my formal training was worth nothing to me.

Chapter 2

The Yoke That Frees

Over the years, again and again, young therapists have come to me for supervision, complaining:

> I'm stuck. For a while the work was going well, but now we're at an impasse. My patient has reached a pleateau. He (or she) is blocking and I can't seem to get him over his resistance. I've tried and tried to figure out why he's doing that but he's fighting me all the way.

At times like these it's difficult for the therapist to understand that "a therapeutic impasse" is simply a time when the therapist is trying to make a patient do something that the patient is not ready to do. By focusing on the patient's "progress," the therapist engages in a needless power struggle. Getting hung up on how well or poorly the therapist is doing also distractedly drains his or her own creative energy from the Work. The most ready resolution for these deadly problems is the therapist's shifting focus onto the therapeutic techniques. Getting out of that awful stuck place requires that the therapist turn attention away from the patient's behavior, away from concern with self-image, and toward concentration on simply doing impeccable work.

The best model I know for getting unstuck is the release from bondage provided by the discipline of Yoga, "the yoke that frees." Though I no longer meditate regularly, the freeing discipline of Yoga serves me well as a metaphor for getting beyond being stuck in trying to get my own way in working as a psychotherapist (as well as in the rest of life).

I remember my own early instruction in the Yoga of breath-counting. To prepare myself, each day I was to sit comfortably for short periods at regular times. My mind would be cleared by focusing all of my attention on the edges of my nostrils; at that place where the breath is exhaled.

My guide told me: "You need only breathe in and out quietly

13

and regularly, concentrating on that point. Each time you exhale, you count to yourself, 'one . . ., two . . ., three . . .,' and so on. When you get to ten, begin again."

That certainly sounded easy enough. But my guide went on to warn me of the demons with which I would struggle: "You'll find that you begin 'one . . ., two . . .,' and then the thoughts will come. And so it will be 'one . . ., two . . .,' and suddenly you'll think 'This isn't working!' At that point you must go *back to one.* You try it again: 'one . . ., two . . .,' and all at once 'Now I'm getting it.' *Back to one.* Still other thoughts will arise to distract you. Discomforts and temptations will emerge as distractions. ('My legs are getting stiff' or 'My ass itches,') and temptations ('I wonder what it would be like to go to bed with that woman I met yesterday,' or 'Someday I'll be truly enlightened.'). Each time you need only go *back to one.*"

At first I did not see why *I* would have to go back to one. All I would have to do would be to overcome those thoughts. As if reading my mind, my guide went on: "You'll be tempted to try to dismiss the thoughts, to simply get rid of them. That won't work. It's just another trap. All that will happen is that you'll get deeper and deeper into your insistence that you can overcome the struggles. The only solution each time is to go *back to one.*"

It began to sound *not* so easy. I started out with the notion that I was certain to go through the series up to ten and begin again. I could do series after series. Should I count them? "Not to worry," said my guide. "During the first year of breathing meditation most people do *not* get beyond four or five. And then come the thoughts, and again it's always *back to one.*"

So it is in the practice of psychotherapy. Again and again the therapist's willful attachment to how he or she is doing, to how the patient is progressing, to the results, to getting his or her own way. All arise as distractions from the work. In each case the solution is to go *back to one.* But first the therapist must have prepared a setting in which the basic work can be done. What's more, he or she must have a clear idea of what is to be done and how to do it, or else there is no "one" to which to go back.

This book is a detailed description of how I do therapy. I offer it only as a guide. These are not *the* ways to work. They are simply *my* ways of working. They need not be yours, though some may suit your own path. I offer it to encourage you to become ever clearer about the fundamentals of *your own* style of work.

To free oneself from the bondage of attachment to its results, it is necessary to be clear about the Work. When we do not concentrate one-pointedly on the basic work, we pay attention instead to the patient's "progress," or to our own ego-bound "Look how well (or badly) I'm doing" trip. Neither path benefits the patient or the therapist. At the point of impasse, the only thing that helps is to go *back to one.*

But to find your way back, you first must know what "one" is *for you.* Clarity about what you do, about how you run the therapy is absolutely necessary. It is sometimes useful, creative, and fun to vary from the basic parameters of your work. But first you must know the personal baseline from which you are varying. Otherwise how can you know when to return home, and how to find your way back?

Learning to go *back to one* by returning to fundamentals of the Work, the therapist is helped to feel comfortable simply being in charge of the therapy, leaving the patient to be in charge of his or her own life. Out of this comes the best work; that *alliance in the absence of blame* in which healing can occur. It is only then that the therapist can offer the expert services of a professional guide, and so avoid the impasse born of the presumption of thinking that the therapist knows what is best for the patient. By concentrating on the therapeutic work the therapist gets unstuck, leaving the patient free to discover what he or she wants out of life, how to go about getting it, and at what cost. It is the patient who must choose just how he or she is to live. When the therapist helps the patient to be happier without needing the patient to change, the therapist's own impeccable work will be reward enough.

So it is with the practice of Yoga as well. Each seeker at first practices Yoga as a path toward the goal of spiritual liberation. Initially taken on as a means to an end by the beginner, the burdensome efforts of self-discipline are later pursued for their own intrinsic rewards by the more advanced Yogi.

Certain aspects of the practice of Yoga can serve as effective metaphors for the work of psychotherapy. Many Westerners think of Yoga as nothing more than a peculiar system of breathing exercises accompanied by grotesque physical postures. Classical Yoga practices are something more than holding your breath and standing on your head. They have little to do with the Americanized popularization of Yoga as a gymnastic cult of physical beauty and prolonged youth.

Some Westerners imagine that the practice of Yoga is an Oriental form of magic, a vehicle for the attaining of occult powers. Not that special powers do not accrue for the Yogi. Rather it is simply that these *Siddhi* are not what they appear to be. The notorious Indian rope trick is a good example of the cheap magic practiced by fakirs who use Yoga powers for exploitive purposes.

Some years ago an account appeared in the Chicago Tribune[1] telling of two Americans who witnessed such a performance while travelling together in Northern India. They both watched as the rope appeared to unwind itself vertically toward the sky. Just as the conjurer's assistant began to climb the rope, one of the Americans who was an artist made a rapid sketch of the scene. His companion, who was carrying a camera, photographed what he saw. Later the photographs showed only a crowd gathered around the fakir, with the boy beside him, and the rope at their feet. Nothing had been suspended but the judgment of the audience. Suggestion or induced hallucination? Perhaps. Levitation? Not according to the photographic evidence!

Among the other Siddhis or "marvelous powers" which develop in the practice of Yoga are those phenomena which we in the West categorize as *para*psychological: extra-sensory perception, telepathy, psychokinesis, and perhaps even outside-the-body trips. They parallel the altered states of consciousness and dramatic instant emotional catharses induced in patients by some Western psychotherapists.

The Indian writers who believe that Siddhis exist, view them as distractions from the right practice of concentration and meditation. Sri Ramakrishna calls these by-products mere "heaps of rubbish"[2] the only importance of which are as obstacles to enlightenment and stumbling blocks in the path to liberation.

Before the publication of *Tales of Power,* an anecdote began circulating in Berkeley, California, about Carlos Castaneda's recent visit to Yogi Chen, an elderly Chinese practitioner of esoteric Buddhism who is something of a local saint. Castaneda, it seems, told Yogi Chen that he was now being taught how to produce a "double" of himself. Was there anything similar in Chen's traditions? Of course, said Yogi Chen, there were methods for producing up to six emanations of oneself, "But why bother? Then you only have six times as much trouble."[3] Equivalent psycho-therapeutic "magic" creates similar distractions in the treatment process.

How are we to understand a path of self-development that considers the acquisition of the power to perform miracles as no more than a trivial distraction from spiritual discipline? This is not true of Yoga alone. None of the Indian philosophies and mystic techniques has either Power or "Truth" as its goal. The West may pursue Progress through Knowledge and Power. The East seeks only deliverance from struggle.

Yoga of one sort or another may be found in all Eastern spiritual paths. In each case the goals are the same: the raising of con-sciousness beyond the distinction between the watcher and the watched; awareness free from desire. The goal is no less than total deliverance from needless struggle through the non-attachment of knowing that *concern with making things happen is meaningless.*

The acquisition of knowledge and power in the absence of the benign detachment that comes with spiritual maturity is a hazardous stage in any path of self-development. The hazards are most vivid in those paths that involve the mastery of violence. Here are some instructive words from the pen of a black belt adept in the Japanese martial art of Karate:

> I think that the most dangerous time for most Karateka [students of Karate] is when they have reached the brown belt level. At this grade, they are strong and fast, and notoriously rough in free fighting. They are accurate with their blows, and deliver them with power, certainly enough to maim or kill. They have learned to focus, and they have begun to learn fighting spirit. All of this they have learned, but they have not learned calmness and tolerance and the state of empty-mind that is brought about by further intensive practice.[4]

The cautions offered by this master of "the gentle art" of Karate hold for the practices of Yoga and psychotherapy as well. Once young therapists gain an understanding of personality dynamics and a repertoire of disarming therapeutic ploys, they enter a dangerous phase. Their focused need to change the patient takes precedence over an unattached readiness to offer the excellent expert techniques which provide an accepting atmosphere within which the patient might grow at his or her own pace. It is a time of struggle between therapist and patient, of therapeutic impasses, and of needless suffering for both.

Understanding the discrediting of such powers in the context of Yoga begins with the Indian conception of life as a "wheel of sorrows" turning from birth through the suffering of this life to death and rebirth into yet another round of pain. As Buddha proclaimed: "All is anguish, all is ephemeral."

The misery of human life is due to the *ignorance* that attributes substance to the illusion that is this life, and to that *attachment* which leads us to try to hold onto the impermanent things of this life. To whatever extent we focus our longing on getting our own way, on doing in order to achieve results, on holding on to things beyond our control, to that extent we are trapped in needless suffering.

Paradoxically, the Indian conception of universal suffering does *not* lead to a pessimistic philosophy founded on despair. Suffering is not a tragedy. It is a cosmic necessity. Yet each person has a chance to become free of it. For each individual, Karma is the crucial pivot.

Karma is the conception that each act has consequences. Our circumstances in this life are the consequences of actions in earlier lives. How we live in this life will determine what our next life will hold in store. It is *not* necessary to believe in Reincarnation to apply this view to our own lives. Even if we have only one life, we create our Karma as we live it.

We can gradually liberate ourselves from needless suffering. It is possible to effect future Karma by doing the Work on my Self of raising my consciousness beyond the ignorance of attachment to the results of my efforts. I only get to keep that which I am prepared to give up. In Western terms, Virtue is its own reward. There is no hope of redemption in doing Good in order to be saved. Only by doing Good for its own sake, without seeking reward, can I attain Salvation.

For the patient, psychotherapy may be seen as an attempt to improve Karma in this life. The therapist helps the patient to heighten awareness of the consequences of actions and of the price of willful attachment to getting one's own way. In part the therapist offers this in the role of the guru who shows the patient ways to unhook from old patterns by the liberation of self from attachment to the neurotic past.

The therapist offers not only the enabling practices of treatment techniques, but the model of non-attachment to the results of his or her own therapeutic efforts as well. *Both* the practices and the non-attachment are crucial to the process. Baba Ram Dass describes the Karma Yoga of such offerings by saying:

> . . . *the only thing you have to offer another human being, ever, is your own state of being* . . . everything, whether you're cooking food or doing therapy or being a student or being a lover, *you are only doing, you're only manifesting how evolved a consciousness you are.* That's what you're doing with another human being. That's the only dance there is! . . . Consciousness . . . means freedom from attachment . . . You realize that the only thing you have to do for another human being is to keep yourself really straight, and then do whatever it is you do.[5]

How can Yoga help us to find deliverance? Indian philosophy provides two avenues. The earlier pathway of self-development is called Samkhya which means "discrimination" or liberation through knowledge. Samkhya provides a basic theoretical exposition of human nature. If a person is devoted in good faith to the acquiring of this metaphysical knowledge, he or she *may* become liberated.

But Samkhya serves as a pathway to release from spiritual bondage only a few rare individuals. For most of us it serves as a preliminary preparation for the real Work of the practice of Yoga itself. Classical Yoga begins where Samkhya ends. It stands as practice to theory, as act to thought, as reality to fantasy.

The term "Yoga" derives etymologically from a root meaning "to bring under the yoke." Yoga offers the seeker the opportunity to unify his or her spirit with the universal soul, to become one with the Way of life by experiencing an arranged curriculum of self-training in ascetic and meditational practices. It is at the same time both a discipline of austerities and a path of liberation. So it is that Yoga is *the yoke that frees.*

There are two primary divisions of these practices, Raja Yoga, the royal path of cultivating the mind and the personality, and Hatha Yoga, the mastery of breathing and other physiological functions which aims at liberation through purification and development of mastery over the body.[6] In attempting to develop a metaphor for the non-attached practice of psychotherapy, I have focused almost exclusively on Raja Yoga, the Yoga of the will, particularly on the practices of meditation, and on Karma Yoga, the way of action and loving work.

Meditation begins with *concentration*. At first this sounds simple enough. All that you have to do is to fix your attention on a single point. It might be on the tip of the nose, on a thought or an action, on a holy saying, or on an image of God. This simple exercise turns out to be enlightening in its unexpected difficulty.

> . . . it's like trying to take an elephant that has been wild in the jungle and putting one of those iron bands around its leg and then sticking a post in the ground to tame it. When the elephant (like your wandering mind) realizes that you are trying to tame it, it gets wilder than it ever was at its wildest in the jungle. . . . It pulls and it pulls and it can hurt its leg. It would break its leg, it starts to bleed, it does all kinds of things before it finally gives in and becomes tame. And this roughly is the tradition of meditation.[7]

It is *not* possible to pursue the meditational path of liberation without straying. Concentration in the practice of Yoga, psychotherapy, or any other spiritual folk art is a matter of developing the ability to *do one thing at a time.* In the practice of meditation, straying from this goal has been characterized as "itching, twitching, and bitching." Because most psychotherapy lacks the physical demands of yoga, and because it is interpersonal, the distractions with which therapists must struggle are more focused on needless evaluative comparisons between how the therapist is doing and how he or she should be doing, or on the reciprocal point of how the patient is progressing and how the therapist thinks the patient should be progressing.

Nonetheless, the problems are fundamentally the same. It is easy for the practitioner of Yoga or psychotherapy to think of other things, to become distracted with remembrances of times past and of other places. Or concentration may be lost by straying into future concerns about how this is all going to turn out. Again, the required correction is *back to one*.

Even seemingly present-oriented self-consciousness serves as a distraction if there is any element of comparison embedded within it. Comparisons are always deadly, whether they pivot around how I am different or the same as another, or merely around how I am different now than I was or will be at another time. The *Law of the Good Moment*[8] holds for the practices of both meditation and psychotherapy. In either case the danger of distracting myself from concentration in the moment is best expressed by the self-competitive thought: "Here I am, wasn't I!"

The goal is to have your whole being concentrated in what you are doing at the moment. Saint Anthony said it well:

> The prayer of the monk is not perfect until he no longer realizes himself or the fact that he is praying.[9]

So it is that when the therapist does the best work, he or she does not experience trying to change the patient, or even experience doing psychotherapy. The therapist *becomes* the Work. The therapist *is* the psychotherapy and it all just seems to flow. The irony is that when the work goes this well, it is difficult to recapture in retrospect just what it was you did right.

A parable of Sri Ramakrishna demonstrates that first we must learn to concentrate and only then may we gain a sense of what it feels like to be doing impeccable work:

> A disciple once came to a teacher to learn to meditate on God. The teacher gave him instructions, but the disciple soon returned and said that he could not carry them out; every time he tried to meditate, he found himself thinking about his pet buffalo. "Well then," said the teacher, "you meditate on that buffalo you're so fond of." The disciple shut himself up in a room and began to concentrate on the buffalo. After some days, the teacher knocked at his door and the disciple answered: "Sir, I am sorry I can't come out to greet you. This door is too small. My horns will be in the way." Then the teacher smiled and said: "Splendid! You have become identified with the object of your concentration. Now fix that concentration upon God and you will easily succeed.[10]

For most of us just one lifetime does not seem long enough

to attain a state of perfect concentration. In our work as psychotherapists, as in our personal lives, we will get distracted, make
mistakes, and lose our way again and again. We must learn to
give ourselves permission to blunder, to fail, and to make fools
of ourselves every day for the rest of our lives. We will do so
in any case. Scolding and self-recrimination are no more than
further errors. Instead we can turn toward the unconditional
self-acceptance of one of India's greatest discoveries: consciousness
as a witness. To do this you must simply try to:

> treat yourself as if you were a much-loved child that an adult was
> trying to keep walking on a narrow sidewalk. The child is full of
> energy and keeps running off to the fields on each side to pick
> flowers, feel the grass, climb a tree. Each time you are aware of
> the child leaving the path, you say in effect, "Oh, that's how children
> are. Okay, honey, back to the sidewalk," and bring yourself gently
> but firmly and alertly back to *just looking*. . . . "Oh, that's where
> I am now; *back to work*."[11]

Le Shan's "back to work" is my "back to one." His "just looking"
is a reminder that if we are to tame the wild elephant of the
mind, we must not beat it.

We recognize that at first it is not easy to get used to staying
in one spot. Wildly resisting by struggling to be somewhere else
is painful and self-destructive.

But willfully trying to force the elephant or the mind or the
patient to stay calmly in a place in which any of these are not
yet ready to stay is also an exercise in futility and needless suffering.
Instead we must learn to witness the discomforting interruption
and the tendency to stray, without longing, with our coercion,
and without blame.

> . . . when it comes up—it's like somebody who drops by for tea
> when you are trying to work on a manuscript. You say, "Hello,
> it's great to have you. Why don't you go into the kitchen and have
> tea with my wife (if she's not busy, too), and I'll be along later.
> I'm working on this manuscript." And then you go back to the
> manuscript.[12]

Whether it's the manuscript or the meditation or the work of
psychotherapy, at such times you simply go *back to one.*

Chapter 3

The Fundamental Requirement

Unlike the techniques of the yogi, no matter what the attitude of devotion, those of the psychotherapist cannot be practiced without first establishing a relationship with someone who will take on the role of the patient.

Most books on psychotherapeutic technique begin with a discussion of the setting in which it is to be practiced. Clearly, comfort, privacy, and lack of distraction are all helpful, but psychotherapy can be conducted in all sorts of settings. The presence of a patient is the only necessary (though not sufficient) condition for the therapist's practice of this particular folk art.

Though I now work in a lovely private office complete with reclining chairs, carpeting, and original wall-hangings with a wide-windowed view of trees and the sky, my early work was done in less elegantly facilitating circumstances. As a very young therapist I saw patients in correctional institutions. The administration considered the Work to be a luxury at best (and at worst, "inmate-coddling"). So it was that some psychotherapy sessions took place in solitary cells with one of us seated on a cot and the other on a primitive toilet. In one over-crowded reformatory, the only place in which I could work was the corner of a gymnasium while a full-court basketball game was in progress.

The first prerequisite is not *where* but with *whom* psychotherapy is conducted. The first issue is that of *referrals*. My model for most of the discussion in this book is the private practice of individual psychotherapy. There are special problems involved in the coercive therapy of institutions and the bureaucratic therapy of agencies.[1] The special advantages of both these settings is that they provide staff therapists with patients.

Almost all therapists begin their work in institutions or agencies. Eventually many of them move on to the private practice of psychotherapy. The immediately-posed problem is how to get patients with whom to work. The earliest practices in this field

23

involved therapists being trained by psychoanalytic institutes which then took responsibility for providing patients for the graduated analyst. Helpful as this might be, both economically and in terms of keeping the analyst's posture "pure" and filling the need for patients, it does require that the therapist never develop too far beyond what the Institute regards as orthodox acceptability (lest he or she kill the goose that lays the golden eggs).

The young therapist moves out of agency or institutional work to operate independently, to make more money, or to get out from under the oppressive constraints of the System. He or she rents office space, gets malpractice insurance, and sends out embossed announcements that a private practice has been set up. Then the therapist waits. It's a drag. Nothing happens.

The therapist gets depressed, sometimes tries to hide a sense of failure, but finally begins to complain. In supervisory consultation with me, there is much talk of dissatisfaction with sitting alone in that empty office. "What can I do?" "Where are all the patients?" the therapist asks.

After checking out what has been done so far, I point out that the two necessary (though not always sufficient) conditions for getting referrals are *visibility* and *trust*. The therapist must become known to the referring community, and must somehow project an image of competent and responsible work.

There are many ways to become visible. They include doing consultations with public and private agencies in the community, offering voluntary services to the "free community," giving talks at churches, luncheons, PTAs, and the like. Most important is asking other therapists for referrals. Usually the young therapist will tell me that this is all too bold and presumptuous at this stage of the game. To go out and hustle for the work seems too daring.

I always find this ironic. Too humble to hustle, the beginner has the arrogance to sit quietly in a private office waiting to be discovered by the world. I offer assurance that this posture is not entirely without merit. Some people do get discovered. If it's not just a press-agent's story, Lana Turner was first discovered while sitting at a drug-store counter on Hollywood Boulevard sipping a coke.

However, should the ordeal of sitting around and feeling sorry for oneself become tiring, I suggest going out to make a claim on the world. True, there is the risk of active rejection under those conditions. But if the therapist has something to offer, perhaps referrals will be made. This is especially likely where we work.

In the Washington metropolitan area there are more therapists per capita than in any other city in the world. Because of the government agencies, insurance coverage, and the like, it is very easy to make a living in private practice in this part of the country. As the young therapist begins to brighten in response to this I go on to point out that even bum therapists make a living in private practice in this town. And so it is that if the practice blossoms, he or she may be happier and economically more secure, but it will offer no definite assurance that good work is being done.

When I began to set up my own practice in Washington, my shyness made it painful for me to go out to give talks or to attend public functions. Instead I came to depend largely on my writing as a way of heightening my visibility and offering some image of my work. It became my way of letting people come to know me so that they could judge my trustworthiness.

In addition to my books I turn out three or four journal articles a year. I always order a few hundred reprints. Without waiting for requests I send out a reprint to each of the people and agencies on my mailing list. This up-to-date card file includes a few friends, my "fans" (people who correspond with me about my writing), and all the individuals and groups in the area who might make referrals to me. This often seems presumptuous to the young therapist who insists that there is no point in self-exposure in the absence of absolute certainty that people will be glad to know of his or her existence.

I go on to explain that I have been in private practice for almost 15 years, and that by now I usually get many more referrals than I need. Still from time to time I too am faced with the problem of needing new patients. The practice threatens to collapse twice a year. Patients terminate around the therapist's vacation time, sometimes because that fits their own psychic schedule, and sometimes as a way of acting out against the therapist's abandoning them. The other time when many patients leave therapy is during the Thanksgiving–Christmas family depression time. (A sub-set of Jewish patients act out this way during the High Holidays.)

During these lean periods I talk to the few therapists whom I see regularly, telling them that I am in need of referrals. I may send notes to a few other colleagues with whom I have worked in the past. The young therapist is usually astonished that even now I would still have to ask for referrals at times. It may even seem degrading for me to do so. This has to do with a grandiose projected image of that time of success so great as to be beyond problems; a time when the world is at one's feet.

It is not surprising to me that arrogance is a matter to be discussed again and again with therapists in supervision. It's presumptuous enough for anyone to decide to become a psychotherapist in the first place, to put oneself in the position of helping another person with the unsolved personal problems. Too often there is a temptation for the young therapist to believe that his or her own problems should already have been resolved before taking on the role of helper, healer, and guide.

Personal therapy for the therapist is a helpful hedge against an excess of self arrogance. The experience of being patients ourselves helps immeasurably in understanding what those who come to us for help are going through. Working through many of our own problems and getting some perspective on the rest of them offers protection to our patients. It makes it more likely that we will be in a position to understand them and less likely that we will exploit them to ease our own psychic pain. But the work on the Self takes more than one lifetime.

In the beginning, setting up a practice demands that the therapist solve for the moment the problem of getting referrals by becoming known to, and trusted by the referring community. Eventually, if the work goes well, former patients will refer other people. Ultimately, this pyramiding network is the most reliable and most satisfying groundwork for an ongoing practice. Some psychoanalysts object that such referrals contaminate the work with the original patient. Their idealized standards of purity are practical only because of their institute-based life-time referral sources.

Initially the therapist must look to the therapeutic community for referrals. Social and personal contacts cannot be depended on as a source of patients. There are some patients whom no therapist should treat. These include people with whom the therapist has a social or personal relationship, and others who are intimately related to people with whom the therapist is closely involved. There are also patients who might well be treated by some therapists but not by others. We each need to know what our own preferences and limitations are. But this is a problem of patient selection, not of referral.

I am no longer willing to treat patients who seem too difficult to me. In no case will I take on a patient whom I believe I cannot help. There is already enough in my life about which I can do nothing. Voluntarily committing myself to situations in which I will inevitably be helpless and despairing is foolhardy and irresponsible.

Because of the way I work I will not take on patients whom I expect will be moving in and out of mental hospitals during the work. I neither do good work nor do I like to put up with following them in and out of that system of warehouses for debilitated human beings.

When I began working in this field, I preferred treating people who were functioning so poorly that they could not stay out of institutions. In retrospect, I see a large part of my initial motivation as my wanting to work with problems so difficult that my own limited competence would not be revealed by meager results. Now I am more likely to select well-functioning people who are too hard on themselves; individuals for whom the focus of therapy is more a matter of growth than of problem-solving. Great patients make great psychotherapists, so perhaps my motivation has not changed as much as I like to believe it has.

A therapist first beginning in private practice is not yet in a position to be very selective about which patients to take on. When I first began my own private practice I asked a training analyst with whom I was in supervision what my criteria should be for selecting patients. His answer was: "Time enough when you are earning a living and have many to choose from. For now if a gorilla walks into the office with a ten dollar bill clutched in his fist, tell him to lie down on the couch."

Paradoxically, there is an irony of timing involved in patient selection. The more a therapist gets a reputation for *not* taking on just anyone who comes for an initial appointment, the more referrals come in, and the more ready many patients are to choose that particular therapist. Early in the practice is the time when the therapist most needs the patients. At that time, he or she is least likely to dare to maintain the most effective posture, that of not accepting every patient who comes for help.

Once a patient is referred, there must be ready access for making contact with the therapist. A 24-hour switchboard or answering service works best. The therapist's name may be listed in the Yellow Pages, but this is for the convenience of those who have already been given the name. Self-referred patients who pick out names from the classified section of the telephone directory are usually unsophisticated, upward-mobile people who naively expect instant cures. If the initial emotional crisis passes, they usually do not show up for their first appointment. I have come to refuse such referrals over the phone, suggesting emergency services or community clinics where that seems appropriate. One index of the outlook of such people is the therapist I know who seems to get more of these calls than any other. I believe he does so because he has the symbolically promising name of Dr. Jewell.

Though I have a telephone within reach in my office, it is important to me that therapy sessions do not get interrupted by incoming calls. My way of solving this problem was to get the phone company to disconnect the bell, replacing the ringing signal with a flashing light. The light is positioned so that I can see it but the patient cannot. That way I know that there will be a message for me in the lobby. I have instructed the people who run the switchboard to ask for nothing more than a name and telephone number from the caller. Time enough to find out what the message is about when I call back.

The only time that the switchboard operator is to buzz through for me to pick up the phone is if there is an urgent call from my wife or from one of my kids. There are no other emergencies in my profession. I only run the therapy, my patients run their lives. Should patients attempt to make their emergencies mine, I accept no responsibility for intervening in their crises. At such times of distress in their lives, just as I do, they must turn to family, to friends, or to community crisis intervention services (such as the police, the fire department, the local hospital emergency room, etc.)

Typically a phone message from a prospective patient will read

"Mrs. Mary Smith, wants an appointment" plus her telephone number.

When it is convenient for me, I return the call, saying: "Mary Smith, this is Sheldon Kopp." Deliberately, this takes the first contact out of the traditional doctor-patient mode, posing us as social peers, stripped of hierarchical titles, and leaving the relationship undefined in a way that requires a conscious choice of salutation by the caller.

I do not deal very well with telephone contacts, either professionally or in my conversations with friends. Put off by the mechanics of the transaction, and by the absence of personal presence and eye contact, I feel awkward and am often described as being impersonal and abrupt on the phone.

My intent is to try to hear where the patient is emotionally. I try to remember that the caller will be even more anxious than I am at the moment, and that he or she may have little prior basis in experience for beginning to make contact with a stranger about personal problems.

I listen to what is offered with an ear for any communication about what sort of person I am dealing with, and what the expectations about me might be. In particular I try to be alert for indications of strong reluctance, uncertainty, and conflict about making the contact. I may even make a brief intervention, but it will be lighthanded and not presume more understanding of the patient than has been communicated.

Should the patient begin to discuss personal problems, I interrupt at the first natural break and try to limit this in a way that is responsive to the implied motivation. For instance, I might interrupt gently with: "There's no need to justify yourself. You can come to see me if you wish"; or "You seem to want to let me know just how upset you are. I hear you. Let's talk about it when you come in"; or "It sounds like a complex struggle you're having. We'll make better sense of it once we get a chance to sit down together and talk it over."

There may be indication of conflict about an appointment time. I offer an appointment if I have free time. This may include a choice of one of two open hours, but it is a firm offer without accommodation to any expressed needs that might serve as reluctance to letting me stipulate just when I am available. (I never work evenings or week-ends, keep a regular 25-hour week, and make no attempt to appease prospective patients by giving in to their demands that I see them at their convenience rather than my own.) If the patient balks at the inconvenience of the proffered hour (many do), I am ready to offer to recommend some other therapist. Most patients do find some way to work out being able to make the hour I offer. In this way we resolve the patient's initial demand for any ceremonial accommodation on my part.

Should the caller ask about my fee, I suggest that it is something we can discuss when we meet. If he or she is insistent, I answer: "It doesn't really matter for the moment. I won't charge you for the first visit unless we both decide to go on and work together." This is usually sufficient to discourage any further struggle with that bit of reluctance at the time. The patient is often surprised, pleased at the openness of the arrangement, but at the same time may be put off by the way in which this dispels the illusion of control. As for myself, it is simply a way of feeling free to spend the first hour exploring whether or not I want to work with the patient without my having to feel under any obligation to provide any service during that session which would conflict with this initial exploration. As there will be no charge I am also free to end the session at any point should I choose to do so.

During this initial telephone contact, I always ask: "Who suggested that you call me?" Whether or not I have time open to offer an appointment, I want that information so that I can maintain some overview of my referral-source power-base in the community. I want this information at the outset because even if I do set up an initial appointment, the prospective patient may not show up. Only one out of three patients who get a referral to a therapist ever follow it through even to the first appointment. Fewer than that work out. This may be my only opportunity to learn the referral source.

If I do have time, I make sure that I have the spelling of the person's name (if it is ambiguous), and that I get a mailing address. This is simply a matter of getting these administrative billing details out of the way on the phone as a way of avoiding their disruptive, trivially business-like impact during the first session.

If I do offer the caller an appointment it is in the context of saying: "I do have a free hour to see you. Would you like to come to my office so that we can sit down to talk together? That way we can find out if we like each other well enough to work together." My emphasis implies a context in which as free agents we will chose one another (or not), and that this will depend entirely on what it is like for us to be together.

If I do not have time, I say so. I do *not* immediately offer a substitute therapist. Instead I ask if the caller would like the name of another therapist. Sometimes the patient already has some names and still wants another. At that point I simply suggest going ahead with the names on the list with the option of calling back should none of those work out.

In the traditional manner, I used to give three names. My inclination now is to give just one. I will respond to the patient's living or working in a certain far reach of town by offering a nearby therapist if I can. I will also respond to a patient's stated preference for a psychoanalyst or a Gestalt therapist, or something of the sort. I offer a name without guaranteeing that this therapist will fill the expectations of the patient. However, I do try to pick therapists whom I know have time, and only refer callers to therapists whom I know to be competent.

When I do not have time I ask if the caller wants another name. Some insist that I am the only therapist that they want to see. They may have either heard some things about me and are determined to see me in particular, or are simply set to get their own way. How long would they have to wait before I have free time, they may ask. My answer is always the same. I state that I do not know when I will have free time. It might be soon or it might be a long way off. I do not keep a waiting list.

I go on to respond briefly to the caller's expressed feelings. I might say, "I hear the disappointment in your voice," or "Getting your way certainly is important to you." Nonetheless if the caller persists I also suggest that if the issue is trying to get his or her life to a better place, it seems foolhardy to me to wait for a particular therapist. There are many other therapists who could help. But I leave it up to the caller to decide.

When someone does persist in calling me back in a few weeks and then again a few weeks later, that sometimes seems reason enough for me *not* to offer an appointment even when I do have time. Such a person's stubbornness, and need to get his or her own way simply gives too much up-front promise of power struggle in the therapy should we choose to work together.

The patient may ask for instructions as to how to get to the office. I keep these very simple, indicating only where the office is located. Should the patient begin to ask what bus to take, where to get off, and the like, I offer an intervention about my impression that there is a feeling that we will not meet unless I agree to give instructions each step along the way.

Some patients let me know that they are calling because of an emergency, and that I must see them right away. I have learned never to take on patients who meet me in that way (at least not on *their* terms). In the past when I have met such cries for help, it has resulted in crisis after crisis, with my initial behavior confirming their illusion of emergency and rescue. Instead I offer the patient an hour the following week (which is what I would have done with any new patient).

If the patient accepts the appointment, that's fine. We will surely discuss this "emergency" during this opening session. If not, I suggest that the patient can try some other therapist (in which case I do *not* give a name) or suggest that the emergency room of a hospital might be contacted. Sometimes patients persist about how they are on fire at the moment. I must come and put them out. It sometimes seems enough at those times to ask, "How long have you been unhappy?" The response usually is something like, "Ten years, but it feels really awful this week." At that point we can sometimes laugh together and the patient is assured by my not going bananas over the uproar.

The identity of the person who has referred a patient to me is of obvious economic and professional interest. In addition, the nature of the referring agent is of clinical significance. It allows me to tap into some intuitions about what preliminary transference fantasies the new patient may bring.

It is important to find out by the first interview if this person has been referred by someone who is or has been a patient of mine. In that case, the new person's expectations will be contextually embedded in the reported experience of the referring patient. At other times the patient has been referred by another therapist, which might simply mean that there is a background of disappointment in not being given an appointment by the therapist of choice. It may indicate the patient has been going through the ordeal of therapist-seeking with the frustration of finding that one or more people have not had free time.

Another source of new patients for me is the self-referral of someone who has read my books. While this would suggest the possibility that the new patient would come with some realistic expectations about whom I might be, it is just as often loaded with fantasy-filled response to my writing.

The referral source may also define my own expectations. When I was a young therapist, a referral from a supervisor or from an established member of the therapeutic community whom I greatly respected often carried with it a self-demand that I do an especially good job. If I have a personal relationship with a referring therapist or agency staff, then some of that emotional matrix will also color my sense of what I am about when I first meet the patient. Or I might have a background of experience which suggests that this particular referring agent makes "bad" referrals—patients with whom I have difficulty.

There are some times when the first telephone contact comes from the referring agent. Another therapist may call me and say that he has in mind a person who is an ex-patient or at least someone who is known to that therapist. The caller may want to let me know that this patient is being referred especially to me (thus setting up a network of implicit demand of reciprocation from me when I receive this "gift").

My usual response is: "All you have to do is give that person my phone number. We can take it from there." I refuse to discuss the matter further. There are times when I have to be brutally direct in closing off any flow of information about the patient. Though the data may be offered to be "helpful," it only serves to burden me with the gossip of personal information that the patient has not given me directly. It serves as a secondary source of subjective distortion. This is a chronic problem in mental health agencies that routinely "screen" the new patient through one or more intake workers. The therapist is then burdened with their reports before ever meeting with the patient.

I myself never contact the therapist to whom I am referring

a patient. Nor do I go to any special trouble to facilitate the patient's getting there. It would seem disrespectful to attempt to take care of either of these other adults in that way.

In any case as a therapist it behooves me to explore within myself the counter-transferential elements in my reaction to the patient within this context of feelings and fantasies about the nature of the referral and the relationship with the referring agent. Examples from the unwanted feedback I get on referrals to other therapists include: "She was a real gift"; "I can see why you couldn't stand him"; "I was pleased when I realized that you saw me as competent enough to handle that complicated referral," and the like.

For what I take to be social and political reasons, some therapists routinely acknowledge their having received each referral. At times this gratitude is communicated in the form of a bread and butter thank-you note. This is a position of weakness. If someone refers a patient to me it is *not* a present, it is an acknowledgement of trust. That therapist is lucky that I am there to receive referrals. The list of therapists to whom I refer here in Washington is a selected group of perhaps a dozen and a half names and numbers. I enjoy the chance to send referrals to talented young therapists who are just finding their way. But a referred patient is *not* a gift to them. Rather, it represents my own delight at the convenience of being able to find some few more people in the field whose work I trust.

For each therapist the problems implicit in the meaning of particular referrals occur again and again. Once the therapist gets established and maintains an alertness to their occurrence, these problems become less frequently troublesome and for the most part, low-keyed. That has been my situation for the last several years until another particularly vivid experience let me know that, though useful, having enough referrals is not sufficient protection in every case.

This particular experience involved referrals from Carl Rogers. Though Rogers is a man whom I only have met once briefly at an American Academy of Psychotherapists workshop, for many years his writings and tapes have instructed me and moved me deeply. His work has shaped some of my attitudes as a therapist, as it has so many workers of my generation in this field.

Carl Rogers is a profoundly human, incredibly gentle psycho-therapist whose major contribution to the field is Client-Centered Psychotherapy. His focus is on the *person* of those seeking help. He offers "unconditional positive regard" and respect for the way in which the client experiences his or her own situation. His non-judgmental tenderness has been an inspiration to many of us. It has served as a much-needed corrective to the medical model of pejorative clinical-diagnostic judgments that preceded it.

Two or three years ago I was working with a patient who was professionally and personally involved with Carl Rogers. One of this patient's problems (or perhaps I should say one of his costly solutions to his problems) was to lionize people who inspired him, turning them into substitute fathers who were bigger than life. Curt military leaders, and later, gurus of the human potential movement (including Carl Rogers) became super-heroes for this man. Part of our work together included my facilitating his demythologizing his transference-exaggeration of my own worth.

During one session late in our therapy relationship, this patient reported a dream of which he has written in one of his autobio-graphical books on Humanistic Psychology:

> A final dream that I will share involved a meeting at my house of General Maxwell Taylor and Carl Rogers. (I had actually invited Carl to be my guest just before dreaming this dream.) In the dream I was very eager to show off my very precocious and independent children to Carl. However, when he arrived in the dream, neither he nor the children were very much interested in each other. The children went about their playing, and Carl decided to walk out in the backyard. I felt a little disappointed, and then General Maxwell Taylor arrived. But, hard as I tried, neither he nor the children showed any interest in each other either. After a while I looked out the window, and there in the backyard were Carl Rogers and General Taylor, sitting on a bench in animated conversation with each other. I then thought, "That isn't so strange. They are both in their seventies. They are both fascinating men who have accomplished significant things in their lives. Why shouldn't they both be more interested in each other than in me or my children?" I then realized how different they were: Carl almost a pacifist, General Taylor a brilliant but strong advocate for the military.
>
> Upon awakening, I knew I had been like both men in my life, and I was both men in my conflicts. Certainly it would be easier to be only one and not both. My impasse—my stuck place—is somewhere between the two of them.[2]

The patient went on to write of how he understood the dream and of how we worked in that session with the residue of the identity-struggle to which it spoke. In the service of helping the patient to further demythologize his hero figures, I suggested that he might share this dream with Carl Rogers. I implied that perhaps it would be helpful to Rogers in getting in touch with the General Taylor who was struggling somewhere down inside of him.

The patient later reported that he had followed my suggestion. In so doing he heightened his awareness of the struggle. This helped him further in keeping others from looming so large in the panorama of his life as to limit his sense of his own power.

Out of this transaction came an unexpected consequence for me. Soon thereafter, Rogers began referring patients to me. I was startled to find that I was still crazy after all these years. Once more I was impressed with the importance of the meaning of the referring agent to my expectations about the patient. No doubt the dream work with my own patient and my suggestion to him in the attempt to facilitate his demythologizing of Rogers, was in part an instance of continuing the work on My Self.

This became clear to me when I realized that just because the referrals came from Carl Rogers I found myself feeling flattered. Once more I discovered that I was anticipating having to do especially good work, and expecting that these referrals would turn out to be absolutely wonderful patients.

It was instructive to learn from my telephone contacts with these patients that they were a perfectly ordinary spectrum of referrals. As a matter of fact none of them worked out. I never did get to see any of the three or four people whom he referred.

I understand this now to be a combination of two limiting conditions of referrals of this sort. Having gone to Rogers because of his super-reputation, the patients found it difficult to settle for someone else. Additionally Rogers operates from somewhere out on the West coast while I work in Washington, the contacts had limited probability of being completed. All such cross-country referrals of recently uprooted people involve individuals making a quick grab at settling-in. It is often unlikely that they will follow through with this desperate and often premature security measure.

My first response to these innocent people was to react with an unwarranted sense of well-being, to their saying that Rogers had referred them. In each case, almost immediately thereafter, I found myself disappointed that this did not seem like a particularly fascinating prospective patient. These spontaneous irrational responses served as further proof that even practicing a good opening therapeutic posture over many years is no guarantee that I will not again and again be distracted from the concentration needed for the Work.

Chapter 4

Assuming the Posture

My own early training as a psychotherapist was strong on theory but weak on practical guidance. This imbalance was partially corrected by my personal experience as a patient in psychotherapy. But for the most part, there was little direct instruction on just how and what to do when working with a patient. The confusion, needless suffering, and delayed competence that followed from this lack of preparation in my own early work contributed to my motivation in writing this book.

As I begin the chapters on technique, it seems fitting that I start with a discussion of the therapist's basic stance in meeting a patient for the first time. Assuming the right posture puts me in the best position to offer the help I promise. Some future impasses are avoided in advance, or at least made less likely to occur. Others that may be inevitable are met more readily if I am already in a well-centered position.

In the practice of Yoga, the basic posture is called *asana*. To the beginner, asana becomes the first problem to be solved in the initiation into the practice of meditation. The instructions alone are intimidating. To achieve *padmasana*, the easiest and most common meditative position:

> Place the right foot on the left thigh and, similarly, the left foot on the right thigh; cross the hands behind the back and grip the ends of the feet (the right hand on the right foot, and left hand on the left foot). Rest the chin on the chest and focus the eyes on the tip of the nose.[1]

In the beginning the asana is uncomfortable and even intolerable. But after a while it becomes "stable and pleasant" (Patanjali).

After a time, effort disappears and the meditative position becomes natural. At that point for the beginner, posture stops being a distraction in itself. It is gradually transformed into a foundation that facilitates concentration in the adept.

The therapeutic asana is already implied in the posture for obtaining and accepting referrals. It is more clearly defined in the beginning of the first hour. Then it is to be carried out throughout the course of therapy to the end of the last hour, and beyond. It begins as a preparatory attitude for the later work. At the same time the comfort and stability of a well-centered position facilitates liberation and impeccable work. The therapist need not understand the theoretical underpinnings to benefit from the posture. Whenever I find myself straying from my basic asana, I need only go *back to one.*

When it is time to begin the first session with a new patient, I am usually curious, excited, and somewhat scared. If the patient shows up before the time we have agreed to start, and I am free, my spontaneous impulse is to get right to it. This would seem most natural with a patient who arrives early and seeing my name on the door, comes directly to my office. Instead, I send the patient to the waiting-room until the appointed time.

Beginning early would involve my acting out my impatience in order to avoid the inner stirring of my own unsettled feelings. I will need this heightened readiness when we do begin *on time.* In the interim, the unresolved turmoil can be examined so that I may better understand my fantasy expectations about this particular patient.

In addition, the error of beginning early would mislead the patient about the parameters of our agreement. It would encourage the feeling that the therapeutic hour could begin whenever the patient chose without regard for having to contend with me as a separate human being, or with my necessary therapeutic posture.

And so I wait, alone, in my office, coming to the waiting-room to get the patient only once the exact moment of the hour's previously agreed-upon beginning arrives. I enter the waiting-room, identify the patient by name, and say: "I'm Sheldon Kopp. Come on in." At this first meeting, I shake hands only if the patient spontaneously reaches out for such contact. Any insistence on the patient's part of our continuing a social greeting in future hours will be analyzed.

I escort the patient to my office. It is a large informal living-room arrangement with two couches, a few chairs, and several lamp-tables and coffee-tables. There is an alcove off to the side containing a writing-table and chair, file cabinets and book-cases. At the far end of the room are two large, upholstered reclining-rockers at either end of the picture-window that dominates the room. They face each other at an angle and are obviously set up as the most likely arrangement for a face-to-face conversation.

The pipes and other personal effects on the table beside one of the chairs makes it clear that this is where I usually sit. Not so obvious is the fact that its placement allows me the most facilitating position to compensate for the deafness of my left ear. In addition, the angle at which it faces the companion chair permits me comfortably either to look directly at the patient, or to gaze off into space without giving the impression that I am uninterested. I let the patient find his or her way to the chair to be used for the interview without unnecessary direction.

The patient takes a seat and I allow a minute or two to look around and see what the office is like. If the patient does not begin to speak (and many patients do not) I begin by asking: "How can I help you?" I do not expect the patient to be able to tell me just how I can help at this point. However, the answer to that question gives me some sense of the patient's state of mind. For example, some of the kinds of replies which the question often elicits include: "I'm not sure just how you can help me." "I'm not sure anyone can help me." "I know that I really have to help myself."

A new patient often finds it difficult to begin to talk to a stranger about problems experienced as overwhelmingly complicated. My response is usually supportive in acknowledging: "Of course it's hard to begin, but you can start anywhere. It's all attached."

I try to follow wherever the patient seems to be going, commenting on the expressed feelings without analyzing them. My initial mode is simply to reflect back what the patient is saying in order to communicate the sense that I am actively listening and, where possible, that the patient has been understood. If I can, I simplify the vision of what the patient is experiencing at that point, attempting to help bring it to manageable proportions.

I attempt to create an atmosphere during this first hour that is one of my acceptance of what the patient chooses to present. My posture and attitude are meant to communicate my interest in getting to know the patient, and my willingness to let the patient get to know me. I do not take a history, preferring instead to allow circumstances of the patient's life to evolve in a natural sequence. This unfolding will be determined by *the patient*'s needs and experiences rather than by some preconceived notion that I have about personal development or clinical pathology.

I am attempting to get to know something about who this person is, what hurts, and what resources are available for dealing with stress and pain. Where I can, I share small bits of my own experience and response in order to let the patient begin to know who I am.

By the clarity and directness of my responses, I show the patient that I know what I am doing. By allowing the story to unfold in the patient's own way and at his or her own pace, I also attempt to communicate that I believe that the patient knows best how to provide the other half of the dialogue.

The safe, nurturant ambience that evolves is one in which nothing that is said will be met with criticism, punitive confrontation, or a tone that indicates that the patient is doing anything but exactly what it is he or she must do at that time. If we are well-met, the patient will come away with a sense of having done it all just right, and that I am completely satisfied that we have each done just what we needed to do with each other.

Later in this first (or perhaps second) hour, once we have established an initial picture of what the patient is struggling with, I will state my professional opinion. I offer my expert judgment as to whether or not what the patient is describing is the sort of problem for which therapy might prove useful. Approximately one out of ten patients describe presenting problems which do not seem to call for therapy at that time.

If the patient is seeking therapy to resolve a political situation such as avoiding the draft or pre-empting a criminal charge, I will not offer treatment. If the patient is there under duress, sent by someone else in the family, I suggest that the other person is the more likely patient (unless there is a stated wish to explore the need to comply with family demands).

Sometimes the presenting problem is more one of vocational choice, or some other developmental choice-point. If the normal sense of stress and mixed feelings that accompany such transitions do not seem embedded in more general problems of inner turmoil and self-limiting life style, I make this clear. I then may go on to suggest that the support this non-patient needs might be more readily and less expensively available in an everyday life situation.

Some people come with a detached wish for what they believe to be the educational rewards of therapy, but without the needed inner pain which foreshadows change and growth. A young psychotherapist called me one day to ask for an appointment, saying that he was not sure whether he was coming for supervision or for psychotherapy for himself. The appointed time came. He seemed very self-possessed. By then he had decided that he wanted both supervision and psychotherapy. He chose to discuss the issue of supervision first.

He talked lucidly and straightforwardly of his wish to learn to do better work. Knowledgeably clear about where he stood in his own development as a therapist, he understood what sorts of things he now wanted to learn. It all made sense to me. I liked him and thought him a promising professional. We agreed that I would take him on for supervision on a weekly basis.

Next we turned to his interest in getting psychotherapy for himself. I asked him how I could help him. He replied that he felt that to become a truly competent psychotherapist he would first need the experience of being a patient. I concurred that that made sense and asked him what personal reasons he had for going into treatment. He answered: "I'm really pretty happy and function quite well, but I don't believe that I have yet actualized my full potential as a human being. Psychotherapy will help me to do this."

I replied: "That's fine, but where do you hurt?"

He could give no response that was not inferential. He could only say: "I guess if I'm not working up to full potential there must be something I haven't yet dealt with."

I told him that we could go on with the supervision as he had requested but that I did *not* take anyone into treatment unless that person had highly personal motives. Some other therapist might feel differently about this. I would be glad to refer him to another therapist for his own treatment while I supervised his professional work. He seemed both disgruntled and relieved at my offering this arrangement, but did not accept the referral. "I guess supervision will have to do for now," he concluded.

The supervision went well as we moved from contract and technique to his feelings about the patients with whom he was working. Finally, some three months later, in the midst of a supervision session, I shifted attention from his struggles with his patient's dynamics back to his own sense of helplessness. For the first time he began to cry. All the feelings about his helplessness in his relationship with his father came pouring out.

I responded to how pained and helpless he was still feeling and then said: "Now we can begin with your treatment." From that point on he was in individual therapy twice a week while continuing his supervision once a week for as long as that was needed.

It may become clear to me during the course of the first hour that though the patient could use therapy, I do not wish to do that work myself. Or the patient may not care to work with me. I am quite serious about our choosing each other. I cannot assume in advance that either of us will want to spend time with the other. The patient has to decide whether I seem competent and trustworthy, as well as just what it feels like to be with me. I must decide whether or not the patient seems to need therapy, and whether or not I believe I can help. Beyond this, it is crucial to my own well-being that this person be someone whom I believe could become personally important to me. I am no longer willing to spend hours of my life with someone whom I do not believe I could come to care about.

The patient's need for therapy, coupled with my confidence that I could be of help are necessary but not sufficient conditions to my choosing to do the work. If I do not choose to work with that person I communicate exactly on what basis I am making this choice. The most likely response is that of feeling rejected. My answer is: "That's an accurate perception. I am rejecting the possibility of spending time with you because it does not feel wise to me to be with someone I don't expect to come to mean a great deal to me. I do want you to understand that I believe you are showing good judgment in seeking therapy at this time. There are many other competent therapists who might be happy to work with you. I will not charge you for this session and I will give you some other therapists' names if you want them."

This sort of transaction is hairy, but far less destructive than the patient later having to contend with my feeling stuck. Rejection sometimes hurts, but it does not damage the way inauthentic acceptance can. Most important, this choice is best for me. My first responsibility in my work, as in the rest of my life, is to take good care of myself.

During the initial interview, I will also ask (if it is not offered spontaneously) what fantasies the patient had about what our first meeting would be like. Some of these will need to be sorted out in terms of what expectations were set up by the referring agent (such as "He's a good therapist," "He will help you," "He doesn't see everyone," "He may not have time," etc.). Or it might be set up in terms of a particular aspect of my writings which the patient responded to personally. It may have to do with the matter of reputation ("He's a tough therapist," "He's very intuitive," "I know somebody who saw him and had a terrible time," etc.).

If the patient and I seem to be moving toward an agreement to work together, I raise the question of frequency of appointments. Beginning by expressing an interest in the patient's wishes I ask: "Setting aside for the moment the practical problems of time and money and of my availability, if it was entirely up to you, how often would you like to come to talk with me?"

The patient's answer as well as the tone and form in which it is expressed will be examined. Responses may range from the deeply hungry reply: "If it was up to me I'd like to come every day, and just stay and stay," to the reluctant-to-ask-for-too-much: "I suppose once a week would be enough if I worked really hard." At times more than anything else the patient's answer is an expression of understandable mistrust of a stranger by someone who has been hurt too often before: "Well, maybe once a week at first. Then after a while, if it works out all right, we could begin to think about whether my seeing you more often would be a good thing."

I respond to these comments by reflecting my understanding of the patient's feelings and opening them to exploration of related experiences in therapy and in other relationships. In addition, I go on to offer some explanatory structure about my conception of frequency. I might say something like: "The availability of time and money are real issues but beyond these, frequency is essentially a matter of how much of our opportunity to get to know one another we are ready to take on now. The most important consideration is how well we like being together, and consequently how much time we would be willing to spend with one another. Another aspect for me is whether you feel good enough to tolerate the intimacy of our being together frequently. That's just too hard for some people at first. I will set a minimum for how often we meet. It will have to be often enough for me to feel that we might be able to get somewhere. There's too much in my life over which I have no control; things I'm just stuck with. It doesn't make any sense to me to take on any unnecessary despair. So if you want to work with me you would have to agree to at least a minimum frequency within which I could feel hopeful about what we are doing. There are no guarantees about the outcome, but I do insist on spending time with you only if I feel the set-up will allow me to do my best work. In your case, I will be willing to see you a minimum of . . ."

At that point I might stipulate once a week, twice a week, or three times a week. With a patient who seems too frightened for rapid self-revelation, I usually begin by inviting him or her to come once a week. The same might hold with a patient who is as yet vague about what is being sought. I would first give such a person the chance to explore what therapy is to be about for him or her before asking for any large commitment. In the case of patients with complex problems, elaborate character defenses, or such overwhelming suffering that neither of us could manage to face the pain in so fragmented a fashion, I insist on seeing the patient at least twice a week. Patients who do a lot of acting out, evoking recurrent crises in their lives with friends, at home, and at work, may also require more frequent contacts. Otherwise we could spend one hour administering first aid each week, our work would be limited to exploring that week's crises without ever moving beyond them into what there is within the patient which necessitates all this furor.

I listen to the patient's response to my proposal, paying attention to both the realistic problems that attend such a commitment, and to the conscious and unconscious emotional conflicts about our coming together. Making the patient aware of these attendant reactions often serves to resolve them as barriers. If this is not possible, I simply will *not* take on a patient who insists that he or she cannot come to see me as frequently as I require for the bottom line to doing excellent and hopeful work. This is *never* a ploy. The patient must accept the minimum frequency which I stipulate, or I will offer referral to another therapist. This will be done without criticism or blame, and indeed at times with expressed regret on my part.

If the patient is uncertain as to whether or not to choose to work with me under the conditions which I set out, I encourage trust of that distrust. Rather than pushing for a decision then and there, I suggest waiting and thinking it over after the session. If the patient doesn't want to continue or cannot decide, he or she only need not bother to call me back within the next two days and there will be no charge for the initial session. (I make clear that after that I cannot promise that I will still have any free time open.) The patient can keep whatever has been gotten out of our meeting. At the same time $50 can be saved. Should the patient decide to go on, picking up the phone to call me will cost $100 (half for this session, and half for the next one). I do not want to spend time with anyone who does not want to be with me enough to overcome the barriers I put in the way.

Carl Whitaker taught me the value of raising the ante with reluctant patients. If Carl insists on the phone that a man bring his wife with him for the first interview, and the man balks, he ups the ante by demanding that he bring his children as well. Any further resistance is met with Carl's letting him know that some other therapist might not insist on all this, but Carl's next move will be to add the demand that the dog accompany the family to the interview. Patients either decide that Carl is crazy and go find some other therapist, or give in before he asks to see the neighbors as well. In this way the first problem of the nature of the therapeutic alliance with a therapist who has such a powerful asana is resolved *before* the first meeting.

If the patient is defending by hedging against contract demands, I too increase the demands. I stipulate a bottom line of one session per week. The patient wants to come less often, and is met by my increasing the minimum to twice a week. If the patient wants to try it out for just a couple of weeks, I insist that a three month commitment be made. The patient is free to leave without charge or to stay in a context within which I can do impeccable work.

Either alternative is acceptable to me.

> One problem that does arise is the issue of good faith in such a resistant patient. That is, I may get him to agree to a three-month twice a week trial period in psychotherapy, but he might have in the back of his mind that if he doesn't like it he is going to drop out anyway, and there's nothing I can do about it. In some cases I solve this power struggle by insisting on getting a retainer as part of the contract. The patient is, of course, suspicious, feeling that I might somehow do him in and push him to break the contract so that I can keep the money. In order to double-bind him around that issue I set up the retainer as money which he will indeed lose if he breaks the contract, but *not* as money that I will gain. For example one such patient recently was a Jewish man married to a Catholic woman with whom he often passively struggled. He was unwilling to make a commitment; I insisted on a retainer of two hundred dollars in the form of a check made out to Catholic Charities, payable only if he broke the contract.[2]

Some of the people who come to see me live alone. Others still live within their parental families, or have established new family configurations and are sharing a life with a husband, wife, or lover. I find that when early on in the work I meet the people with whom the patient shares a life, it makes it easier for me to evaluate how hopeful I feel about working with that particular patient. There are times when working with the patient seems promising only because I have not yet had direct contact with the counter-therapeutic mate with whom he or she is joined in a deadly misalliance.

Before finalizing any agreement to work with the new patient I stipulate routinely that the "other half" be brought in for at least one joint meeting, usually in the second session. For many patients this is no problem. Others balk, most often explaining that the mate would not be willing to come. We explore why *the patient* might not want the mate to come by my inviting a fantasy about what it would be like to ask and by what might happen if the other person did come. This is easily clarified by encouraging imagining what is hoped would be the best way it could work out, and then what is feared is the worst that might happen. At first it surprised me that when I made this claim on new patients even the balky ones usually found a way to bring in the significant other.

Once all of this has been established, if we are interested in working together I take up the issue of the therapeutic contract. These ground rules of psychotherapy usually are stipulated in the closing minutes of the first hour. It if seems necessary to have a second joint hour with a mate (or parent), this exposition may be delayed until the beginning of the third hour. I keep this presentation as simple as possible, knowing that further clarification and renegotiation may be necessary in subsequent hours should any aspect of the contract resurface as a problem in the therapeutic relationship.

Explanation of the contract is usually stated in the following way: "We are agreed that we want to try working together to see if I can help you to be happier. I will offer you a regular appointment hour (or hours). I can see you Wednesdays at 3 o'clock in the afternoon." At this point we deal with whether or not the patient can make that hour. If it is inconvenient, we explore what it would take to arrange to be able to make it, plus whatever power pivots or attempts to control might be revealed by this transaction.

I go on to point out: "The therapeutic hour is fifty minutes. This will be your regular hour. I take a month's vacation in August. Aside from that and a few traditional holidays, you can count on me to be here to spend that time with you. Whether or not you show up or arrive on time for every appointment, you are responsible for paying for the hour. I schedule appointments by the week. When you cannot keep a particular appointment, if you let me know I will offer you another time that week if I have a free hour in my schedule. If it's convenient for you, you can have it. If you can't make it, you will still have to pay for the originally-scheduled hour."

Therapists vary a good deal on the handling of charges for cancelled appointments. Practices range from no charge for missed appointments if there is "realistic cause" (translate: a good excuse), to no charge if there is "ample" notice given (24 hours for some, and up to one week for others), to payment for every missed hour with no substitutions or time changes allowed. I suspect that my work will improve when I am disciplined enough to take the latter posture.

There are some clear dangers in too permissive or inconsistent a stand by the therapist. If I do not take good care of myself by seeing to it that I am paid for the time I have contracted to the patient, my resentment will take its toll later in the work. No therapist is smart enough to decide what is a "realistic" reason for the patient cancelling and what is not. If I do *not* charge a fee for absences when the patient claims to be sick, it encourages acting-out through illness by the patient.

In a well-run practice of psychotherapy, few hours are missed. In order to maintain a stable therapeutic posture around contract issues, I need only be able to tolerate the patient's sometimes seeing me as arbitrary, unreasonable, or even hateful. In any case, the basic consideration is that I maintain a clear, consistent policy, so that any deviation can be recognized and understood.

I go on to tell the patient: "My fee is $50 an hour. I bill at the end of the month. Payment is due by the middle of the following month," Should the patient respond in an uncomfortable way to my citing the fee, I point out: "Therapy *is* expensive. I charge more than most therapists in town. If this is more than you can afford, perhaps I can suggest another therapist or an agency whose fee you could manage."

The issue of third-party payments may arise at this point. Should the patient let me know that treatment will be paid for by a relative or by health insurance coverage, I tell the patient: "It's up to you if you want to be reimbursed by the insurance company (or by a relative). Our contract is between you and me. I offer my services to you, and you pay me directly. Whatever you do about getting reimbursed is your affair, and if there is a problem of delay, it's *your* problem." This is one of the many instances in which I make unyieldingly clear the stipulation that as the therapist *I am in charge of the therapy, while the patient is responsible for running his or her own life.*

I then go on to make it very clear to the patient that I have only two rules about what I expect in the therapy relationship. Both involve my own first order of business, taking care of myself: "There are only two rules on which I insist. The first is that you pay your bills on time. The second is that you don't do any damage by hurting me or breaking up the office. Beyond that, when you come here, what you do will be up to you. This will be your time and your space, a place to work or to play, or a place to relax and rest, or a place just to be. If we spend the time getting to know each other, therapy is likely to be of help to you."

This is one of the earliest moments of the development of the ongoing theme of my basic posture with the patient. I will take care of myself. My sole concern with how the patient behaves is promotion of awareness of it, and to making sure that I am not mistreated. The only real damage that can be done to me is by messing with my money, my body, or my property. I do not need the patient to speak to me or to feel about me in any particular way. I certainly do not need the patient to make any particular use of the therapy time. In choosing to spend some hours of my time with this person, I have already asserted that I am satisfied with the patient just as he or she is. Should the patient want to alter the way he or she lives in the interest of greater happiness I am committed to offering expert services to promote awareness of what is wanted and of any self-defeating patterns that prevent fulfillment of those desires.

The patient is already acceptable to me. I don't need the patient to change. I may grow to care about this person, but I do *not* care how he or she lives or what choices are made about living that life. I will do the job of heightening awareness about self and how that life is lived. What the patient does with this increased consciousness is not my concern. My wish is to make myself known to the patient to get to know that other person, and to enjoy the rewards of knowing that I am doing impeccable work. "Progress" in therapy is the patient's affair. If therapy is an educational experience for the patient, it is one in which I begin the work by accepting him or her as a patient. This gives an "A" for the course at the outset. After that, what he or she gets out of the experience, it is up to the patient.

One final matter is taken up, this time not as a rule but as a suggestion. I say to the patient during this first hour, "*When* you decide to leave therapy it would be useful if you came in and talked to me about it at least once rather than terminating on the phone." Here the patient often balks about my raising the question of our separation when we have only just come together. This is an integral part of the Work in that from the beginning we move toward the ending.

I go on: "In return I promise you that I will not put you out of therapy precipitously. If it feels to me like I want to end the work at some point, I will be sure to discuss it with you first. Perhaps we will be able to work out the problem, perhaps not. In any case we are both grownups and free agents. We come together because we want to and we can stop when we like."

The contract is the basic asana of the therapeutic work. When I first began the practice of breath-counting meditation, my teacher would intervene from time to time, to correct my posture by having me straighten my spinal column. He explained that for the yogi, the spine is "the axis of the universe." He compared it to a tree that has its roots in the earth and its crown of fruits in the sky. The posture must be correct for the *prana*, the breath of the spirit, to flow upward freely so that it may nourish the life of higher consciousness.

It is the same with the therapist's maintaining of his correct basic posture. Again and again he will be tempted to stray from his focussed concentration, distracted both by the inner attachments of his ego and by the patient's undisciplined episodic insistence on getting *his* or *her* own way. Each time the therapist must go *back to one.*

Carl Whitaker's clarity on this matter is superb when he writes:

Most of the components of psychotherapy are so ambiguous, so personal, and so loaded that it's hard to have anything that's clear-cut. The one rule that seems relevant is that any administrative discussion of the time, place, frequency, fact of going on with or not going on with appointments has *priority over everything else* and that any effort to push the therapeutic administration around should be dealt with as a mandate for immediate cessation of therapeutic work and a renegotiation of the whole contract.[3]

Chapter 5

Beginnings and Endings

My Teacher told me that meditation was really just "time out." It took a while before I understood what he meant. Faced with the prospect of sitting quietly with eyes shut and nothing to be accomplished, most Westerners fall asleep.

As a way of helping me to learn how to use this special space for time out, my Teacher suggested that I set aside regularly scheduled sessions of predetermined duration. They were to begin and end at the same times each morning and evening. Each meditation session was to open and to close in ritually relevant ways.

A special place in my home was to be selected for meditative sitting, a quiet space in which I was to keep my pillow and timer (the only equipment needed as adjuncts to the primary instrument of my Self). In preparation for the period of meditation, I was to eat just enough so that neither hunger nor feeling too full would serve as a distraction. I was to wear loose comfortable clothes and to blow my nose and rinse out my mouth before beginning. The temperature, lighting, and noise level were all to be optimally comfortable so as not to deflect my attention to bodily needs.

He taught me how to settle into the correct sitting position by spreading the cheeks of my buttocks to an easy setting on the pillow. Next I was to set the timer for fifteen minutes, assume the correct meditative posture, and half-close my eyes to facilitate focusing on some space midway between myself and the wall I faced.

My first session took place in a meditation group at a workshop of the American Academy of Psychotherapists. I assumed the posture and tried to will myself into a meditative state that was to last for 15 minutes. I was skeptical about the whole matter. Without realizing it, I did somehow give myself over to the experience. After a period of time that seemed to last only a couple of minutes, I found myself no longer meditating. I opened my eyes, turned toward the novice sitting next to me whose eyes were also opening.

"I'm just *not* getting into it," I said to him.

He shook his head as if he was having the same experience. Just at that moment the timer bell rang. Fifteen minutes had elapsed. In retrospect I believe that the timer was just a bit slow and that only our internal clocks had been correctly set.

My Teacher suggested that I end each individual meditative session in the same ritualized way. When the timer went off I was never to try to ignore it by continuing to maintain the meditative posture. Instead I was to understand that the "time out" was over. My way back into the space of ordinary life was to gently rock myself from one side to the other as a way of coming off the higher spiritual plane and back into my everyday consciousness.

In their own way, therapy sessions are also time out. Separated from the rest of the ongoing stream of life by a deliberate shift of attention, these sessions have a definite beginning and ending, and rules of their own. This highly focused situation has a quality of heightened experience of each moment. This intense awareness is difficult to retain in ordinary life situations. The patient and I have agreed in advance that we have only so much time together, that each session has an anticipated ending, even as the therapy relationship itself will someday end. It gives the experience that heightened clarity and value that each of us brings to our lives at those times when we are clearly aware that soon we will die.

Like the first meeting, each subsequent session is begun exactly at the appointed time. I enter the waiting-room, make momentary eye-contact, greet the patient with an invitation that is some simple variant of: "Hi, you can come on in now." The patient follows me into my office. From then on until we are seated and the patient begins to speak, I am silent and make no further eye-contact. Before and after the patient enters and leaves my office, I open and close the door myself. This is one of the ways in which I define myself as keeper of the beginnings and endings of our time together.

After closing the door, I cross the room and take my usual seat. Once seated I neither speak nor do I look up until the patient has begun to speak. Instead I sit with eyes closed concentrating

on my breathing. This may last anywhere from a few seconds
to several minutes.

Avoiding eye-contact eliminates our participating in any deferential ceremonial social gestures. This leaves the patient free to get
in touch with what is going on inside at that moment. In the
meantime I practice a Tibetan breathing meditation. It is different
from the traditional Indian meditation of relaxation and dissociation
from the outside world. In contrast this might be understood as
a work meditation. It combines alertness and relaxation.

Simply stated, it involves my quietly attending to my own
breathing in and out. At each inhalation my mind-set is toward
awareness, clarity, and readiness to respond to whatever comes
to me from outside. Each exhalation brings with it an alternate
mind-set of relaxation.

So it is that as I inhale I feel a sense of brightness, sharpness
of focus, and readiness to respond. As I exhale I let my body
relax, feeling a softening of any tensions that might deflect my
alertness away from response to the patient. I often experience
this alternating state of fixed attention as the fresh cool energizing
intake of air followed by the letting out of warm soft air which
has already served to energize.

When the patient does finally speak, I find my attention alert
to both the content and the tone of what is expressed uncluttered
by preconceptions on my part. (If the patient's silence goes on
much longer than usual, I may look up, observe any non-verbal
behavior, and respond to that as the first communication of the
session.)

Patients tend to respond to my initial silence and inwardness
on a number of different levels. These often follow a definite
progression. Early in our work together, any patient who is uneasy
about anticipated rejection often experiences my opening posture
as disinterest or aloofness. Eventually my behavior will come to
be experienced as the silent statement: "I am here. There is no
demand on you." The patient may come to feel relieved to find
so open a space, a time when no claims are being made. It allows
the patient to pay attention to what is going on inside.

Gradually it helps the patient to know that he or she is to be
trusted. In part, it is my way of saying: "This is your time to
get to experience what is going on inside of you. You know best.

Wherever you wish to begin must be exactly the right place for you right now." Much to the patient's surprise, it is he or she who must lead in this self-examination. I guide along the way by following wherever the patient would go.

Meetings and partings are highly sensitized spaces for human beings (just as they are for animals in a forest). Entering and leaving other people's space always involves some instinctual territorial response of invading or being invaded, and of abandoning or being abandoned. Our knowledge of this comes from ethnography and animal behavior.[1] Because of the implied instinctual threat, deferential gestures are required to quiet the powerful internal forces which are stirred by these encounters.

The presence of other human beings offers a continuous challenge to the face we would present to the world. Each of us has been taught to maintain some measure of constraint of our primitive appetites, to present at least the appearance of sociability and self-control. The virtues of good character (however they may vary from group to group) are supposed to be in evidence. Some element of respect for the other, of cooperation, of candor, and of modesty are expected. A certain modicum of civilized demeanor is demanded, as we play out the masked dance of social accommodation.

We are to act as though we were not driven by powerful biological urges, not haunted by dark primitive images, as though our social identities represent who we really are. In order to maintain this acceptable sense of theater, social interaction is replete with ceremonies, conventions and ritual dialogues which preserve the gloss of civilization.[2] Infractions and deviations which either intentionally or inadvertently reveal our underlying primitive natures are subject to censure, and quickly corrected by remedial interchanges. So it is that the powerfully primordial mythic images which guide human behavior remain hidden behind a facade of mannered reasonableness.

. . . psychotherapy is an effective interruption of old behaviors partly because of the therapist's willingness to operate without engaging in such remedial work. His personal transparency combines with his limiting his participation in protective social ritual. Unchecked by such constraints, the therapist and patient are plunged into primitive personal intimacy, surging with the emotional power of their surfacing transpersonal mythic patterns.

From the very beginning of his contacts with me, the patient is faced with ambiguities which resist resolution into familiar social categories. My style of meeting is largely free of the ceremonial lubricants which ease most social interactions. Wherever possible I avoid the ritualized manners which so often afford the appearance of civilized contact of the sort which does not require unguarded personal encounter. The therapist's pointed refusal to provide remedial gloss or impersonal relief does, of course, raise the patient's level of uncertainty and anxiety. This increases the risk of his leaving, but at the same time demands that, should he stay, he will have to deal in more deeply personal and transparent ways.[3]

Gregory Bateson once went so far as to state that most conversation is simply a way of our avoiding murdering one another. Less intense examples are commonplace. Think, if you will, of what goes on when a guest visits and later leaves the home territory of friends or acquaintances. The visitor cannot come without invitation unless there is an established level of easy intimacy which allows the setting aside of these rules of territorial violation. Even invited guests must knock and be admitted. Faced with the disturbed instinctual protective responses to this encounter, greetings are demanded in which eye-contact, facial expression, and conventional verbal exchanges assure both parties that there is no danger in their coming together.

The desert greeting *shalom* means "peace." The handshake or the exposure of the right hand shows that one is not carrying a weapon. And even in the "civilized" suburbs of America the visitor and those who are visited quickly affirm that they are very glad to see each other assuring one another that they mean no harm. The host must offer ritual gifts of food or drink to show that he does not fear that the other has come to take these things. The visitor is expected to accept the gift so that the host can be assured that this token will suffice and that the visitor will not take all that he has.

Only once these ceremonial assurances have been transacted can friends settle into a series of more casually comfortable exchanges. Some time later on in the visit there is another shift. Spontaneously there is an increased frequency of positive statements about the good feelings, the welcome and hospitality, and the ease and enjoyment of being there. These include statements such as: "It's really been a good evening." "I enjoyed being with you." "We need to do this more often." "Be sure to stay in touch." At this point it is clear to everyone that the evening is coming to a close. These deferential gestures are ways of ameliorating the implied threat of abandonment inherent in leaving or being left.

As the guest begins to leave, these expressions and gestures become more intense and more frequent, often ending with an assuring embrace. People usually do not leave quickly. Their hosts participate in making the leaving into a gradual transition. Even though everyone has decided that the evening is over, some time must be spent standing around in final exchange. This is carried on long enough for everyone to feel sufficiently comfortable with the leaving to be assured that their instinctual anti-social impulses will not be openly expressed (nor even allowed to come into awareness).

Should the embarrassment of a replay be called for, the whole transaction is exposed as something of a sham. For example, consider such a warm, wonderful parting of good friends, happy to see each other, and sad to think of parting again. The guests may find themselves outside on the walk or in the driveway only to discover that one of them has left a scarf or gloves. There is an awkward embarrassed feeling at having to return.

Once back on the porch the returning guests knock at the door hesitantly.The host and hostess say to each other: "What the hell are they doing back?" Muted expression of this may be held down to an uneasy glance or a questioning shrug. The door is opened. The guests come back in, apologizing for having left the scarf. At this point if there is any exchange of how good it was to be together, it will be fragmented, abortive, and clearly insincere. The disruptive quality of this return gives the lie to the seemingly totally good feelings expressed at the first leaving.

In conventional social situations most of us tend to make small talk as a way of gradually easing into intimacy. We assure the other of our interest, concern and good intentions by saying, "Glad to see you," "How are you?" and the like. As a therapist I do none of this in meeting with a patient. Early in the therapy the patient may attempt to maintain such deferential social gestures simply as a carry-over from the usual manner of relating. This soon gives way to the immediacy of simply talking right away about whatever is really on one's mind. If not, it must be considered a defensive maneuver meant to avoid more troublesome matters, or an attempt to control the therapy by insisting that I react in reciprocal deferential ways.

During the first few sessions, a patient may tell me what a lovely office I have, begin to chat about the weather, or ask me how I am today. I respond with silence. I may then comment on the patient's reaction to my not offering the expected confirming reply. Eventually I may confront any continuing persistence in the face of my non-response. If there is no hidden agenda, this chatty behavior quickly drops out as the patient gets down to becoming aware of what's on his or her mind.

Over a period of many sessions a patient may persist in trying to push these sticky interactions to the place where he or she wants them to end up. In this case what we are dealing with is character defense in which the patient uses a social veneer to control situations, to please others, to demand reassurance, and to avoid intimacy and self-revelation. My silence as response to these demands and my comments on this style of relating are offered as therapeutic interventions.

For another patient, the pattern may be different. Social exchanges that began early sessions in the therapy soon are abandoned. Even if a patient never displayed that kind of behavior, later on he or she may *suddenly* begin a session with such small talk. This change always means that something hidden is going on. The small talk is then an important defense against highly charged material, usually involving feelings toward the therapist. The intervention of silence at that point is usually responded to by the patient with a negative affect. Reactions may include depression, sulkiness, and complaints of feeling rejected. I may be criticized for being so callous and cold.

I am careful not to attempt to manipulate the patient at that point. I will not inhibit the bad feelings by giving in to demands in any way. Instead I do what I can to reflect that the patient wants something from me which I am not giving. Pointing out that this reaction to my non-participation is very particularized and intense, I wonder aloud what else might be going on.

In a recent meeting of a therapy supervision seminar a situation was discussed in which a patient's seemingly friendly small talk masked serious conflicts. There were no patients present at the seminar that day. One of the therapists came in very upset, reporting that her patient had threatened suicide.

As we explored what had led up to this crisis, the therapist reported that two weeks earlier she had told the patient that they would not be meeting on the following Thursday because the clinic was to be closed for Thanksgiving. She offered to see her for a make-up session on Monday of the holiday week.

The patient had not asked for the substitute hour. The whole matter was *not* explored or discussed during the hour. the patient's only comment was: "That's fine. I'm going to be busy on Thursday anyway."

On that appointed Monday the patient arrived early for her appointment. Atypically, she made a good deal of small talk at the beginning of this session. When the therapist commented on this, the patient insisted that she was only "being friendly" in enquiring about how the therapist was that day, and what plans she might have for Thanksgiving. The therapist did not comply with these demands for a response, nor did she interpret them. Correctly, she withheld any fulfillment of the patient's wish to make such friendly chit-chat. However, by not making the correct intervention of interpreting these comments (or at least exploring them) she left some of the work undone. Instead, she simply waited out the patient hoping that she would go on to more "relevant" material.

That Friday night, the patient called the therapist at home to say that she was very upset and wanted to talk with her. The therapist listened for a while to the patient describing how bad she felt. When the patient threatened suicide, the therapist made a second error by offering the patient an extra hour the following week. By now it was all in a muddle.

The therapist was aware that she had made some mistakes in handling the interaction but she was not quite sure what she should have done. I interrupted to take her back to where it had all begun with this patient. I enquired as to whether or not she had raised the issue of cancelling the Thanksgiving Day appointment at the *beginning* of the hour of the previous Thursday. She had done that. But she had not left room for the patient to respond so that her reaction to the change could be analyzed. Instead, she had immediately offered a substitute appointment to the patient. The result was the inhibiting of direct expression of the patient's hurt and anger at the disruption and experienced abandonment. How could she express those kinds of feelings to someone who was taking care of her by giving her a substitute appointment?

This material did not come up and was not analyzed directly during the substitute hour. Instead the patient acted out in two ways. She hid her anger and attempted to make peace with the therapist by trying to engage her in some superficial fence-mending small-talk. She also tried to get closer to the therapist on Thanksgiving by finding out about her plans for the holiday.

Had the therapist responded by revealing her Thanksgiving plans, the issue would simply have been further obscured. However, the missed intervention, neglecting to interpret this behavior, resulted in heightening the patient's depression and hidden anger during Thanksgiving.

The resultant telephone call represents the patient's insistence that she, by God, *was* going to have contact with the therapist whenever she damn pleased. It also represented a punitive threat to the therapist for not taking care of her. The therapist got frightened and rationalized her need to appease the patient with a "clinically-required" extra hour. She tried to bribe the patient into not killing herself by giving her some extra feeding.

I pointed out that the phone call could have been handled by simply listening long enough to find out if the patient was calling to change an appointment. As soon as the therapist discovered that this was not the case the call should have been interrupted with the simple message that the matter could be discussed at the next regular hour.

In the session prior to the phone call, the opening "small talk" might have been handled in this way:

P: "How are you today?"

T: *Silence.*

P: "Are you going home for Thanksgiving?"

T: *Silence.*

P: "I figured you would be having an old-fashioned family Thanksgiving dinner."

T: *Silence.*

P: "I don't know why you won't answer me. I'm only being friendly. You know *my* family doesn't bother with that sort of thing. I was just hoping that at least *you* would have someone to spend Thanksgiving with."

T: "Last time I told you that I wouldn't be meeting with you on Thanksgiving. You told me that was fine with you, but you seem very interested in what I'll be doing instead of being with you."

P: "I just wanted to find out if you were expected to have a good Thanksgiving with people who love you." (P's tone is hurt and insistent.)

T: "You sound as though you feel hurt. You feel that I am questioning the sincerity of your good wishes for my having a happy holiday."

P: (more angrily) "Well, I think a person should be able to be trusted. When *I* like someone, *I* try to be nice to them and not let them down."

T: "You're becoming aware of how hurt and angry at me you are. You were just beginning to believe that you could trust me to be someone who really cared about you. Now you feel I let you down by deserting you on Thanksgiving.

P: "It's just the same way my mother treats me. She says she loves me, but she's always too busy with her own things to even cook a holiday dinner. I told her I didn't care, that I was too busy to come even if she did. But I know I'll just spend the day being miserable and alone, *as usual*. It'll be her fault. It's always her fault. Some day she'll realize that."

At this point the struggle could have been explored in terms of the patient's transference reaction, her difficulty in dealing with her hurt and anger more openly, and the price she pays for "being friendly" by turning her anger on herself. In this way the patient might have moved toward finding more satisfying ways to get what she wants without having to risk self-destructive acting out of her fantasies.

* * *

Before the issue of the opening exchange arises, there is the question of the patient and the therapist fulfilling their agreement by beginning on time.

Infrequently, over the course of many years of doing psychotherapy, I have on occasion begun a session late. My experience of what goes on is that I have become deeply involved in reading something or listening to some music in between sessions and have lost sight of the time. However, in retrospect, I usually find that it has something to do with what is going on between myself and the patient whose session I have delayed starting.

The other day I looked up from what I was reading between sessions to find that my watch read four minutes past the time that the hour was to begin. I went to the waiting room, invited the patient in. He was silent longer than usual. I suggested that his silence might relate to my being late. It is tempting at such times simply not to say anything, hoping that the patient hasn't noticed that the therapist has begun late. That obscures some of the work that must be done. At one level or another the patient always knows when he or she is being mistreated.

In this case my opening line to the patient was: "You've been quiet longer than usual today. Perhaps it has to do with my having begun four minutes late." The patient's response was: "I was wondering if you were going to say anything about it. When I was sitting in the waiting room and realized that it was past my time, I thought about getting up and bursting in to tell you."

We then explored his understandable anger at not having been treated as I had promised to treat him. We were also able to take a look at why his asserting himself was constrained to fantasy.

If the patient had simply shrugged off my pointing out the lateness of our beginning, I would have interpreted his behavior as an avoidance of letting me know how he felt about this.

Later on in the session, after he had expressed some of his anger and explored some of his constraint, I told him simply that I was sorry. It is important not to offer a premature or flamboyant apology which would pre-empt the patient's feeling entitled to his or her anger. In most social transactions an apology is often made less out of genuine concern for any damage done, than as an ameliorative, symbolic act on the part of the offender. Unconsciously it may be aimed at inhibiting the counter-hostility of the offended party.

I then went on to say to the patient: "If it's not inconvenient for you to stay a little later today, we can run the hour over an additional few minutes so that you will not miss any of the time that you are paying for."

Sometimes it is not convenient for the patient to stay that day, or I may have started late enough so that I would not have had time to make up for it myself that day. Then two alternatives would be possible. We could run a few minutes late on a number of subsequent sessions. Otherwise I must adjust bill so that the patient will not be charged for time with me which had been missed. In either case further analysis of the consequences of these changed parameters would have to be discussed.

If one of us is late, it is most likely to be the patient. If the patient is not in the waiting-room when I come there, I return to my office. I sit in a position from which I can see the patient passing through toward the waiting room from the entrance to the office suite. In the meantime I settle down to read and listen to music. The patient who enters late never finds me pacing in a tense expectant manner, distracted with worry, or irritated at having to wait. In examining the meaning of patients' lateness, one factor which defuses the potential power struggle, is our awareness of how comfortably well I use the time that has been missed.

After five minutes have passed, I go out to the waiting room once more just on the chance that we have missed each other in passing. If the patient is not there I go back to my office for the remainder of the hour. After that it is up to the patient to make the contact.

I never comment on a single lateness of a minute or two. Repeated lateness, coming more than a couple of minutes late, and absences are always noteworthy. If the patient does not choose to discuss such occurrences, I will silently attempt to understand them in terms of whatever occurred in the previous hour. The patient's not mentioning lateness often is an indication that it is an over-determined rather than a circumstantial piece of behavior. The patient's first seemingly "unrelated" comments are likely to offer some clue as to what is going on. I invite exploration of the matter, interpreting the behavior when I believe I understand it.

No matter what time the patient arrives, when the fifty minutes is up, I simply say: "Our time is up for today." or "We'll have to stop now." If the patient is in the middle of a sentence I will allow its completion. However, if the patient tends to ramble on, I interrupt no matter what is going on. This may involve my breaking in at a time when the patient is deeply involved in whatever has caught his or her attention. He or she might even be raging or sobbing at the time. It is then necessary to analyze how the patient begins the following session as a response to my understandably upsetting intrusion.

The patient may bring up some highly emotional or complex matter near the very end of the hour. With five minutes left a long, complicated dream may be introduced, one that cannot even be completely reported in that time. Or some great calamity may be revealed in the final minutes, or some attempted change in our arrangements (such as the fact that the patient plans to miss the next hour).

It is hopeless for me to try to deal completely and effectively with any large issue which comes up late in the hour. Rather, the usual interruption must be made when the time is up. I can expect the patient to respond either directly or with derivative material early in the next hour. At that point I must deal not only with the effects of the interruption, but with the meaning of the patient's bringing up whatever was introduced so late in the hour. If this behavior is repeated the pattern must be explored. Underlying meanings may include a bid for extra feeding, a testing of my capacity for limit-setting or simply a hedge against full exploration of upsetting materials. Nothing that comes up in therapy must be considered to be outside of the therapeutic context. No comment made by the patient or by the therapist is "just business," or without therapeutic meaning. Sometimes one or the other will *begin the hour* by saying: "Before we begin . . ." and then launch into some matter as though it did not call for analysis. The same error can occur if behavior that follows the therapist's announcing, "Our time is up," is not later explored as an instance of the patient's stretching of the boundary of that hour.

The therapeutic context begins when the patient enters the office and does not end until the patient has left. Ordinarily I have ten minutes of free time between sessions. Less than a minute is given to writing up session notes. Almost all the remainder of the time is then free for me to take care of business if I wish, such as returning phone calls, going to the bathroom, getting something to eat, etc. I often give myself over to relaxing, recentering, and clearing my head. Getting back in touch with myself makes me ready to meet the next patient. I may meditate, read, listen to music, or go out for a walk. Occasionally, I will have a brief exchange with one of the other therapists with whom I share a suite of offices. However, too often I find that gets me into some kind of quick-solution, hair-brained attempt to resolve my tension. I feel that this is abusive to the patients and I would rather hold off those therapist-exchanges about unnamed patients that we term "discussing the Work." When needed, it is better restricted to lunch hours, to seminars, or at the very least to more extended coffee breaks.

I never take notes *during* a therapy session. I've tried it in the past. It has always ended up dividing my attention and distracting the patient's. In addition, it makes the patient feel that what was said just before I write something down is what interests me. In this way it misleadingly influences the patient's deductions about how to hold my interest.

In recent years, I have made it a practice *after every* session to sit down at my writing table, open the individual folder of the patient I have just seen, and write a particular kind of process note. It begins with the date of that session, followed by the number of that session in the sequence of the work. Most notes include two or three lines of comments on the major motifs of the session plus some italicized instructions to myself.

My notes following the first one or two or three sessions tend to be longer. They include specific bits of new information such as the patient's age, names of significant figures in the patient's life, and other concrete pieces of historical data which it will be helpful for me to have available. The later notes are set up in the context of my conception of the therapy process. This involves the sense that what the patient produces at the beginning of any given session reflects a response to the residue of feelings left over from incomplete transactions during the prior session.

The adaptive context to which the patient responds with derivative materials may also occur as a function of situations which have arisen in the patient's life between sessions. A sense of my own working process notes might best be communicated by my quoting a random selection of those of three sessions in sequence from the folder of a particular patient:

> June 2, 1975—17th—Patient was "everybody's favorite." Super-confident. Somehow it all felt more like an obligation than a privilege. *Slow down on interpretations.*
>
> June 4, 1975—18th—Dream about a crippled boy for whom everybody felt sorry. *Don't push the patient's understanding of his dream!*
>
> June 6, 1975—19th—Feels that I expect him to understand his dreams. He has not been in therapy long enough for that. I acknowledge that we are reliving his family context. *My pace feels right now.*

Before asking the patient in for any particular session, I *always* first sit down to read my notes from the last session. Doing this puts me back in touch with where we were when last we met. This helps me to be aware of the context out of which the opening remarks of this coming session might arise. The initial productions of any session are often explored and at times interpreted within the context which the notes have recalled for me. Reading them before each hour also serves as a self-supervision process by alerting me to the instructions to myself that I wrote down in retrospect right after the end of the prior session.

Because of the way my office furniture is arranged, after announcing the end of the hour, I have time to get up, open the door, and seat myself at my writing table before the patient has left the room. This gives me clear control over the ending of the hour and vividly underscores its closing. As a result of this de-socializing of our parting, most patients find occasion to discuss directly with me at some later point just what the limits of our relationship mean to them.

Seeing that I always write notes at the end of each hour, many patients develop fantasies about what is written and what I do with the notes. Discussion of these projections provides fertile ground for exploration of feelings of trust and distrust of what I am up to. The fantasies also offer a chance to see more clearly feelings about facing and revealing particular aspects of the self.

If the patient brings it up, we explore all of this as we need to. Then in the interest of greater openness and trust between us, I often offer to read some of the notes aloud. If he or she is interested, I will choose a sequence of notes from a period much earlier in this therapy and read them. In this way, I can restrict the disclosure to materials the patient is likely to have worked through, rather than needlessly add to turmoil about issues still embedded in some current struggle.

When I go to the waiting room to let the patient know that the hour is to begin, I sometimes inadvertently witness some private behavior not intended for my eyes and ears. For example, I may enter the waiting room to find the patient sleeping, crying, or busily engrossed in conversation with a patient waiting for another therapist. When we begin the hour in the office, I will, of course, have the memory of this uninvited witnessing. However, this is private behavior which the patient did not invite me to share. If the patient introduces material related to that behavior, I am, of course, free to discuss the matter. However, if it is not brought up, it would be an intrusion on my part to do so. I would be violating personal boundaries by insisting on meddling in matters which the patient does not choose to make a part of the therapy.

The same conditions would apply when I encounter a newspaper account of something that the patient was doing. The write-up might describe the patient's achieving something in particular, or being in some sort of trouble which he or she has not discussed with me. It seems to me a violation of private space to introduce such matters when they have not deliberately been brought to my attention. The waiting room situation is one in which the patient would come to feel on guard, secretive, or ashamed, alert not to reveal anything to me.

There are unplanned meetings between myself and the patient upon occasion. I may be going down to the switchboard to check my messages as a way of stretching my legs between sessions, or I might be entering or leaving the building, only to find myself in the elevator with a patient. This is sometimes awkward for the patient. There is a temptation to lapse into superficial social exchange, or to try to go on with the work usually reserved for the therapy session. My own personal attitude arises partly out of my shyness. "Social" transactions, as opposed to "personal" exchanges, are difficult for me. I do not value them. I have learned to do without them. If I find myself in the elevator with one of my patients, my behavior is no different than it might be with anyone else. I tend to close my eyes, enter into a breathing meditation, and ignore my surroundings.

The awkwardness for the patient of unexpectedly being with me in a strange unplanned setting is often heightened by my lack of social deferential behavior. When the session begins, such an encounter is likely to set up the adaptive context. It will have raised unresolved anxieties in the patient. If the anxieties aren't too great and the patient is straightforward, then these will be discussed directly and we can explore them for whatever heightened consciousness might be developed out of examining this behavior. If the matter is not brought up directly, it will surely be reflected in the derivative materials that are talked about. For instance, after meeting me in an elevator the patient might begin the session by talking about some other situation in life that was surprising, for which he or she was caught unprepared, or to which he felt rejected or unresponded. At this point I would assume that these derivative materials are unconscious expressions of concern about our encounter.

I might begin by pointing out the motifs in the material which has been presented, such as: "You seem to be talking about how upsetting it is for you to be caught unprepared especially when the person whom you encounter is not sympathetic, who does not take care of you." If the patient is responsive I may go on to make a direct interpretation, pointing out that this is what it must have felt like in the elevator with me. If I know enough about it I might go on to make a genetic interpretation pointing out, for instance, that this was like those times when the patient was faced with the situation brought on by father's demands, and in which father was unsympathetic and unsupportive, etc.

So it is that though the hour has a definite beginning and ending, sometimes we must deal with therapist-patient interactions that have transpired between sessions. If so, we deal, but often it is a sticky business with uncertain boundaries. If I run into a patient in a social situation, I cannot do therapy at that point. Any social exchange will be peculiarly artificial (like running into a secret lover at a P.T.A. meeting or a partner in an underground political conspiracy at a family Bar Mitzvah). That's one of the reasons why it is best to treat patients whom I am unlikely to meet in other contexts. I can do the clarifying repair work to the therapy relationship each time the boundaries are crossed, but it is easier to maintain the liberating time-out quality of the therapy experience when we keep very clear just where it begins and just where it ends.

Chapter 6

Changes

Throughout this book I describe the ways in which I practice psychotherapy in their *ideal* form. I do not work this well all of the time. Sometimes it is simply not clear what it is best for me to do. At other times I know what to do but lack the courage, the discipline, the clarity, or the concern to do it. In still other instances, being with a particular patient in a particular situation seems to require variation from my basic conception of how I work. Out of this last dilemma come both creative variations and well-rationalized errors. In any case, because there will be changes from what I conceive of as ideally impeccable encounters, it behooves me to be clear about how best to make these transitions.

Variations from the basic therapeutic posture must be undertaken responsibly. They are justified only by the constraint of necessity. The variations in psychotherapy have to do with time, money, therapeutic postures, innovations and techniques, and the rules of the contract.

In this book I have set out to describe *my* ways of doing psychotherapy to encourage every other therapist to clarify the guidelines of his or her own practice. These are individual rules and demand individual exceptions. I have attempted to set out the models of working from my own rules with their own exceptions.

No aspect of the Work is clinically pure. The mere introduction of a particular therapist in a particular setting already has some effect on the experience and the psychic productions of any given patient. My own style of work involves letting myself be known as a person. I tell my story as the patient tells his or hers. Certainly this introduces all sorts of elements not germane to the patient's existence up to that point. It leads the patient to see me and the relationship in particular ways which must be explored at any point at which they seem to be directly influencing the course of psychotherapy.

These conditions also hold true in the classical psychoanalytic model. There the analyst relates in an anonymous, largely silent mode. There is no revealing of the person or the analyst. Rather the analyst offers "a blank screen" onto which the patient's transference reactions may be projected. The deprivation and distance which this introduces into the therapeutic relationship must also be analyzed in the process.

Whether the therapist is male or female also enters into the patient's experience of the psychotherapy process. Many practitioners believe that for some patients the therapist's gender is crucial to the outcome of the therapy. This may be viewed in one of two contexts. If the therapy is primarily *supportive,* the therapist or the referring agent takes a managerial role with a patient who is defined as being unable to manage his or her life. The therapist is then expected to provide that which is missing in the person's life (as well as assistance with impaired judgment, emotional control, and other ego functions which are deficient). So it is that a man who has not developed social skills with which to initiate and carry on relationships with women may be referred to a female therapist. His contact with her is supposed to provide the missing experience and instruction. The converse would hold true for a woman who is seen as not competent in heterosexual roles. In that case the male therapist is to provide a sympathetic companion with whom social and personal skills can be learned.

Another variation would be one in which a male patient is purposefully referred to a male psychotherapist. Here he may have the comradeship and positive role-model which can be provided by another man, to make up for the absence of friends and peers in his environment. A woman may be sent to a female therapist with the idea that she will have the support of "sisterhood."

This seems to me to be a problematic assumption because the therapist's attitudes about male/female relationships are probably more crucial to the working through of the patient's problems than is his or her gender. No one grows up in our society with clear, uncorrupted attitudes about such muddled issues as sex (no more than anyone in our culture can be entirely objective about race). It behooves each of us to work through our own distorted views about sexual roles in the interests of having a fuller life. At the same time, politically we can attempt to correct some of the critical problems which dominate our sexist, racist culture. We need to be aware of those parts of these destructive attitudes

which have not yet been outgrown in each of us. The residual
sexism of the therapist is much more crucial than his or her gender
in influencing the patient's own attitudes.

Gender-determined selection of therapist may also occur within
the context of *analytically* conceived psychotherapy. In that case
certain patients will be deliberately referred to a male or to a
female therapist on the hypothetical basis of whether or not the
patient needs most to work out mother-related or father-related
problems. The issue is transference. The expectation is that it will
be facilitated by whether or not the therapist is male or female.

In my experience, the gender of the therapist determines *only*
the *order* in which problems and concerns arise in therapy. A
male therapist *may* tend to evoke father transferences before he
evokes mother transferences. A female therapist *may* encourage
mother-complex feelings earlier in the work with a particular
patient.

An early adolescent is the only kind of patient for whom I myself
would recommend a therapist on the basis of gender. I always
recommend a same-sex therapist to provide a role-model for someone young enough to have not yet established a clear sexual identity.
This matching also helps to avoid needlessly confusing sexual
longings for the therapist arising at an age when the patient might
find it difficult to deal with the intensity of such feelings.

There is another reason why the gender of the therapist is *not*
crucial. The primary focus of the transference will be a function
of the nature of the patient's complexes. A patient with a powerful
central mother complex will project this onto a male therapist
almost as easily as onto a female therapist.

To the extent that the therapist's impact *does* elicit particular
transference reactions his or her gender may be less crucial than
the therapist's personality and work-style. My own feminine aspect
is in ascendance at this time of my life both in my work and
the way that I live. Although I am a man, I tend to evoke early
mother transferences more readily than I do father transferences.

I worked with one woman for a few years whose mother-complex
was central to her troubles and to her way of life. Much of what
she experienced with me came out of this central concern of hers,
supported and encouraged by my own mothering style of therapy.
After three years she left therapy far happier than she had come,

at a time that we both saw as appropriate to her moving on. She was well into her first pregnancy at that time.

A couple of weeks after we separated, she referred another young woman to me, a close friend of hers. The friend and I got along very well and agreed to do therapy together. This second woman was a farewell gift from the original patient. It was also her attempt to feel that she was still in touch with me. I understood that this represented some unfinished work that we had not completed before she left.

A month or so into the work, the new patient began her session one day by telling me that she had a message for me from her friend, the original patient. She said: "My friend had a baby girl last weekend. She told me to tell you, 'Congratulations! You're a grandmother!'"

CHANGES INTRODUCED BY THE THERAPIST

Beyond the impact of the therapist's gender, personality, and work-style, there are some changes in therapeutic boundaries deliberately *introduced by the therapist.*

The still useful concept of changing "parameters of technique" was originally developed in a psychoanalytic context by Kurt Eissler almost twenty-five years ago.[1] His point of view is that a patient's particular life circumstances may necessitate a certain practical measure. However, he goes on, "It is a grave mistake to conclude that this measure has general validity because it has proved its usefulness under special conditions."[2] Any change in a parameter of a technique should be minimal, used for only a short time, and then dispensed with as the treatment returns to the basic technique model. The changes should be introduced only when it is clear that the basic technique model does not suffice. Furthermore, the effects of any deviations from the basic techniques must be analyzed in terms of their impact on the therapeutic relationship.

My own position is: *I do not have any rules about technique which cannot be broken.* Knowing my basic way of working allows me to see just when it is not effective at a particular time with a particular patient. No rule should be broken without good reason. The changing of any parameter must be explored with the patient. It is crucial that I remember that I need only change any particular parameter *just this one time*. I need not continue with a deviation from any particular way of working. Sometimes long after the improvisation, again and again it will be necessary to explore its residual impact on the patient.

In a meeting of a supervisory seminar, one of the therapist-participants reported his uneasiness about a recent transaction with one of his patients. He described his own frustration in working with a rather passive patient who obsessed and obsessed about how he was getting nowhere, seemingly without willingness to discuss anything else. After attempting a number of different kinds of interventions without success, the therapist found himself growing angry at the patient. After some thought about the matter, he decided to express his anger openly. He bawled the patient out for wasting his own and the therapist's time and energy. At first the patient seemed stunned, but with renewed vitality he quickly recovered and began to talk about other, and seemingly more productive matters, abandoning his ruminations about how he could not get anywhere. The therapist was puzzled. The results of this transaction seemed like "progress," but somehow he was uneasy about the whole business.

I told him that I thought he was wise to be uneasy. It turned out that in introducing this change (by making a role-playing intervention) he and the patient had been able to act out an old problem of the patient's without any analysis of the transaction by either one of them.

I offered the hypothesis that this patient had been able to get a strong reaction from one of his parents only by stalling around lethargically until the parent was furious with him. I also suggested that it was likely that he participated in other hostile-dependent relationships in which he passively and ineffectually fumbled around until the other person "proved that he cared" what happened to him by getting angry enough to "straighten him out." The therapist confirmed both these hypotheses.

It then became clear to all of us that the seeming "progress" of the patient was a sort of mini-transference cure. That is, the patient did come to feel better for the moment and began to work productively. But he did this *only* because the therapist participated with him in living out his fantasy that a really loving parent was still around to take care of him. This meant that the therapist would have to get angry with him again and again in the event of future back-sliding.

The patient had *not* come to understand himself in the context of this problem, *nor* had he developed a dependable solution of which he himself would be in charge. Instead the transaction simply supported the patient's continuing ineffectuality, the irritation of people whom he wanted to help him, and his dependency on others to solve his problems.

Though not the best solution to this therapeutic impasse, the role-playing intervention might have been useful. It could be used for the moment to clarify and interrupt the underlying power struggle. However, for this transaction to have had any enduring therapeutic usefulness, it would have been necessary to explore with the patient what this change in the therapist's posture meant to him.

Some changes in the parameters of the Work may occur outside of the context of trying to resolve a particular problem for the patient. Instead they arise out of extra-therapeutic concerns. The most obvious example is that of the therapist's cancelling an hour to take a holiday. Time off for illness and vacations may be seen simply as extended examples of this sort of change of parameter. The meaning of the content is different but the form for dealing with it is largely the same.

I introduce changes of this sort at the beginning of the hour. It is the only instance in which I speak first without responding to any particular verbal or nonverbal behavior by the patient.

Earlier in my work I introduced such changes a couple of weeks before the holiday was due to come up. In retrospect, this seems to me to be an appeasing gesture unwittingly aimed at inhibiting the patient's emotional reaction of rage and/or grief. More recently I have come to work tighter, introducing the issue of the coming cancellation at the beginning of the hour just preceding the holiday. Because summer vacations constitute so substantial an interruption in our meeting, I continue to announce them earlier and expect to engage in extensive repair work to the relationship.

In the case of a holiday, I begin the hour by saying simply: "We will not be meeting next Thursday (or whatever day the holiday falls on)." Then I wait. The patient may speak to this point directly by expressing feelings about my cancelling the hour. We can then explore the matter directly. Instead the patient may, simply nod or pause in acknowledgement and then go on to some other topic. At that point I assume that there will be derivative material in the next utterances. It will reflect the residue of any unresolved feelings about the cancellation. These must be explored. We must all pay our dues, either now or later.

This is clearest when the therapist announces a vacation. Should the feelings go unexplored at that time, they are likely to be acted out during or after the break. If the patient's response has not surfaced and been analyzed, there may be an attempt to contact the therapist during the interruption. The patient may behave self-destructively in a way that indicates the feeling that he or she cannot do without the therapist. In contrast, some patients may attempt to demonstrate that they did not need the therapist in the first place (by returning to old patterns without thinking about the Work at all during the interim break). After a vacation, some patients are tempted to take an equivalent number of sessions during which they will not work on their problems or during which they give themselves over to complaining about other aspects of the therapy. Take three weeks off and some patients will spend the first three weeks after return coming late, obsessing, and otherwise covertly complaining. Far better that this be out in the open.

Some patients leave therapy precipitously after a vacation as a way of avoiding having to face their helplessness. This kind of acting out can usually be preempted by our exploring the patient's reaction in advance.

Another time-change that may be introduced by the therapist is that of letting the hour run over the agreed-upon fifty minutes. It is tempting to go on past the end of the session when the patient is particularly anguished at that point.

This is often a mistake. It is an imposition on the therapist's schedule and one that encourages the patient's getting upset in order to get extra attention. Repeated changes of this kind contribute to the therapeutic misalliance of a shared fantasy that the therapist is there to take care of the patient.

This often comes up as an issue in the supervision of a young therapist to whom it seems heartless to interrupt a tearful patient merely because the hour is over. It is very difficult to sort out those times when the hour is extended out of professional conviction from instances when the therapist is acting out of guilt-avoidance so as not to be seen by the patient as uncaring.

I usually suggest the following exercise in self-discipline: "Stop every session exactly on time for one week, interrupting at the end of fifty minutes no matter what is going on. The following week, watch for materials indicating the patients' reactions to your having worked in this way. During the second week expect a great deal of anger from patients; anger that up till then had been hidden."

Often these new disclosures are enough to help the young therapist to see how anti-therapeutic some over-runs have been. He or she is then in a position to do the exploratory work with patients of analyzing their reactions to these changes. All that is required to add this new dimension to the Work is willingness to tolerate the absolutely crucial dimension of therapy: that *the patient be allowed to hate the therapist.*

There is another advantage to be gained by going through this exercise. Once having undergone this ordeal, the therapist will be in a much better position to know when it is therapeutically indicated to run an hour over with a particular patient. Such changes are less likely to be introduced needlessly, the patient is less likely to be exploited in this way just so that the therapist may be seen as a great human being. Even when such changes are introduced appropriately, they require later exploration as to what they mean to the patient.

It was at a group therapy conference that I became most clearly aware of the ways in which therapists fool themselves about running over at the end of an hour. One of the therapists on the panel was presenting himself as an experienced Clinician and a self-styled Humanist. He was explaining to his enthusiastic audience that *above all* the therapist has to be a Human Being (as though he had an option).

He attempted to demonstrate his own deep commitment to human relationships by telling us that any time something really profound was going on near the end of a group therapy session he was running, he would of course let the group run overtime. When challenged about this by a more traditional therapist in the audience, he countered by pointing out that for him compassion was more important than technique. He explained that his willingness to run overtime with his groups had to do with his deep respect for human interaction.

If something really important was going on, he felt compelled to be "flexible." No wooden white-coated laboratory technician was he. He was an authentic, genuine human being more interested in honest human encounter than in following the rules. His self-admiration was supported by the murmurs of the worshipful younger therapists in the audience.

All at once came a voice from the rear of the room. The man who spoke up was an older, crusty, well-seasoned psychotherapist. He said to the speaker: "You say that for you the important aspects of doing therapy are authenticity and flexibility. I suppose that means that when nothing very genuine is going on in a group psychotherapy session, you insist on ending the hour early."

Up to that point the speaker had been increasingly flamboyant and self-assured. Now he could only mutter in a flustered and uninspiring way: "Why, no! It's against the rules to give the patient less time than he has paid for."

Changes regarding payment of fees, like those concerning the scheduling of hours, are important opportunities for therapeutic exploration. Time and money are two of the few clear and measurable parameters of the therapeutic contract.

I have worked at clinics which charged a minimal fee, or no fee at all. Early in my private practice, I saw some patients at reduced fees. I did this in part out of commitment to the community, in part to be one of the good guys, and in part because I was hungry for patients and lacked confidence that I could successfully compete with more established therapists.

Now I charge the same fee to all my patients, $50 an hour. I fill my need for commitment to the community by offering supervisory service on a voluntary unpaid basis to therapists who treat the poor. The present practices feel far less complicated and sticky than my earlier arrangements.

Even at the ghetto clinic in which I served some years ago, I found that the parameters of my work with patients was much clearer when each patient was charged a fee, no matter how small, and when I insisted that they pay their dollar for missed sessions. It was a long and difficult struggle with the administration of a clinic that saw itself as taking care of people who could not be expected to take much responsibility for themselves.

I saw one young man at the clinic for almost three years. Earlier he had dropped out of college to be hospitalized with the diagnosis of Paranoid Schizophrenia. During the time I was seeing him he had returned to school and was learning to take care of himself. Nonetheless his diagnosis classified him as disabled and so he was not charged any fee for his sessions.

We liked each other and the work seemed to go well. By the end of our time together, he was graduating with honors and had arranged to get a fairly good job. I was leaving the clinic to go into full-time private practice. When he talked of wanting to go on seeing me, I told him that I would be willing to continue with him at my then regular fee of $25 an hour. The salary he now earned made this a fee he could afford.

The patient was outraged at my suggestion. His response was: "If I had to pay to see you, I'd be so furious I wouldn't be able to work with you. This treatment has meant so much to me partly because for me its being free was your way of saying that because my parents gave me so little, you were willing to make it up to me."

I was stunned. Suddenly I realized that a crucial dimension of this man's feelings had never been dealt with in three years of free therapy. I wish I could tell you that I was able to shift ground masterfully, do the necessary analysis of the problem, and continue with the unfinished work under a new contract. I couldn't. Perhaps Theodore Reik was right when he wrote long ago that anytime you learn something really important about the Work, it costs you a patient.

Another patient I saw at the clinic was a divorced working mother who paid $1 an hour. We met on Mondays. One day she told me she would not be able to come for her hour the following week. It turned out that she was spending a long winter week-end in Florida with her ex-husband.

When this was explored two weeks later, I learned that they still were deeply involved with one another in a way that prevented either one of them from forming a new and lasting mating relationship. He bribed her with gifts and money as a way of keeping her attached to him. She encouraged him as a way of continuing the fantasy that she could be a bad girl without losing Daddy's favor.

I explored the meaning of this in our relationship, and raised the fee to the clinic maximum of $5 an hour. When I left the clinic a year later, she continued to work with me. But by this time, she was coming twice a week for individual sessions, she and her ex-husband were meeting with me once a week in de-court-ing sessions so that I could help them to separate, and he was coming in once a week for individual therapy. With no change in their financial status their weekly payments for therapy had increased from $1 to $100.

It is possible to do competent therapy at reduced fees. Such work requires careful examination of what this arrangement means in the fantasy life of the patient. It should never be done in a way that is burdensome to the therapist. If the therapist cannot really afford it, resentment will be expressed unwittingly in the work with the reduced-fee patient.

It is often not possible to know in advance what effects a reduced fee will have on the therapeutic relationship. Sometimes it is not even possible to know whether or not the patient really cannot afford the regular fee. Such matters can be explored in advance of contracting for a reduced fee. They must be re-examined later as related issues come up. It is helpful to let the patient know at the time that the therapist reserves the right to reopen the issue at any time in the future. Further exploration will be necessary. It may even be necessary to re-negotiate the fee later in the therapy.

I once began with a patient in private practice at what seemed like a realistically-needed reduced fee. Soon he was having dreams and fantasies of being my very favorite child. This was explored in terms of his history. It became clear that this was the meaning he ascribed to my "special" fee arrangement with him. It also turned out that he had a "secret" savings account that he had not disclosed to me. The fee was returned to the regular level. He got into a great deal of hidden rage and anguish. The Work went on quite well after that.

The therapist may feel uneasy about raising the fees of patients with whom he has already contracted to work at an originally lower fee. The way that psychotherapy works, should the fees be raised only for new patients, the therapist may find himself living on less money than is needed for another one to two years. Other prices for goods and services go up in line with the economy. Patients expect that this may happen with therapy as well.

When I choose to raise my fees, during the first week of a particular month I will simply announce to each of my patients in sequence at the very beginning of the hour: "As of next month my fee will be x number of dollars per session."

Then, as with the introduction of other changes, I wait. No matter what the patient's response, it will be necessary to explore the impact of my introducing this change of parameter. In some cases it may turn out that the patient really cannot afford the increased fee, that he or she is already managing as well as possible with no realistic resources for extra income. In the service of good faith to our original commitment, I might choose to explore the possibility of continuing to see such a patient at the original fee. Should I do that, it, too, must be examined as a change of parameter. I would also let the patient know that when the increase could be afforded, I would expect us to renegotiate the contract to my new fee level.

Clinic and institutional settings muddy the therapeutic parameters of confidentiality as well as those of time and money. Professional and secretarial staff discuss patients' private business, often with the same air of contempt as those schoolteachers who band together against their common enemy, the children.

During the intake procedures, the patients are asked personal questions by the psychiatrist who does the diagnostic interview, by the social worker who takes a social history, by the psychologist who does the testing, and even by the clinic receptionist. The patient gets confused ideas of what to expect from the therapist when many weeks later the treatment finally begins. The patient expects (sometimes correctly) that the therapist knows all about his or her problems. The therapist is stuck with information that the patient has not revealed directly. It's a mess! Often it has already become so hopelessly complicated that not even a competent therapist can do really fine work with a patient met under such circumstances.

It is absolutely essential that a patient be able to experience the therapy situation as a safe and benevolent setting within which to do the difficult work of self-revealing of troubled and vulnerable feelings. Nonetheless in the context of the temptations to make themselves look important, some therapists tell stories about their patients in ways that unwittingly reveal their identities to listeners.

Some of the most important and most instructive experiences in my own life occur with my patients in the context of therapy. In personal conversations I, too, speak of experiences with patients as a way of communicating something of who I am. In my writing I do so as a way of instructing as well as revealing, and occasionally as an unwittingly prideful self-aggrandizement.

I do have the special advantage of being a storyteller. In whatever tales I tell, I always feel free to change the facts in the service of making a point or of telling a good story. Truth is subservient to honesty in my story-telling. Life is made to follow art rather than to be simply mirrored by it. As Picasso once said: "Art is a lie that leads to the truth." This attitude makes it easy for me, then, to tell my stories about patients while at the same time disguising their identities. In telling such a story I am careful to change the facts of life history, profession, even of sexual identity of the patient.

Although the issue of confidentiality is *not* made explicit by me at the outset in establishing the contract, I will make a clear commitment to the patient when there is any suggestion of anxiety about what is told to me not remaining inviolate.

In the District of Columbia there is one legal exception to this confidentiality. I can be summoned to testify at the Domestic Relations Court when the well-being and custody of a child is in question. At such time both in Washington and nearby Maryland, the Domestic Relations Court Master can rule that privileged communications may be waived as a way of clarifying the judgment about the status of a child in a divorce proceeding.

If anyone calls me to discuss something about a patient without permission, I will not even acknowledge that I am treating that particular patient. The consent of the patient is implicit in a call from the insurance company asking for limited explicit information (such as when we began working together). It is also evident when a family member calls to let me know that a patient is ill, wishes to cancel an appointment, and is allegedly too sick to call me directly.

My own writing and the publications of some of my patients also offer some special exceptions. In a few cases in my own books I have published letters, poems, and the like written by patients. This is always done with their permission. And, of course, the matter must be analyzed for its special transferential implications. In this way it is no different from any other change introduced by the therapist regarding the boundaries of therapy. In a small number of instances, in which the patient was a professional writer or therapist, I have been asked to publish the material over a byline. I respect this and comply. In all other instances such quotations are anonymous.

One other instance in which I feel free to acknowledge that I have treated a particular patient, though without discussing the details of the treatment occurs in those rare, special circumstances in which the patient is himself making a public declaration of our relationship. Over the last few years I have treated a number of artists, writers, and musicians. Some of the writers include accounts of episodes in the therapy in their own books. Once a patient has publicly announced that he and I do therapy together, I no longer consider myself under any obligation to avoid acknowledgment of that simple fact.

After almost 25 years of running groups in conjunction with my work as an individual psychotherapist, I have given up doing group therapy entirely. It was time. It felt right. Perhaps some day I'll feel different about it, but I doubt it. I was an adequate group therapist. Occasionally, very occasionally, my work in group was quite good. But, by and large, I am not comfortable in groups except when I am showing off. That works fine for me in a teaching seminar but it is unfair to patients in a therapy group. Entertainment is not what they come there for.

Part of it, I suppose, is having been an only child until I was thirteen. Being in a group, once again, I feel that I have no natural role except that of being the center of attention, either as brilliant entertainer, or as satanic "troublemaker."

Defining my role in that way, I leave little room for an interpretive appreciation of group process. I neither merge with the group nor do I stand outside it as helpful commentator. Instead, I insist on being the hub of the wheel, doing brilliant individual psychotherapy in the presence of an audience. Having a co-therapist sometimes helps to keep me sane for a while in such a setting. But in the long run I tend to interrupt any action that goes on between other people in the group. I allow it only when I can short-circuit it through myself. Group process is then reduced to input from the patients along the spokes of a wheel of which I insist on being the hub.

I still see the usefulness of group therapy for some patients. Even so, when I did group therapy myself I never agreed to decreasing the frequency of individual hours for a patient in order to substitute a group hour in place of our time alone. Even now in some instances a patient who is in individual treatment with me may at the same time be participating in a group led by another therapist. In such instances I let the patient know that I will *not* be talking about him or her with the other therapist. The integrating of the contradictory aspects of the parallel therapy experiences will be the patient's responsibility, though either therapist may separately help with this work.

If a relative or friend of the patient calls to talk to me about the patient, I will immediately cut off the discussion by saying: "I do not discuss my patients with anyone." I report the conversation to the patient, explore its implications, and may offer the patient the opportunity to bring in the "concerned" caller for a joint session if they both wish to have one.

This brings up the one other exception to total confidentiality which I set forth in my work with patients. This limitation to complete privacy occurs in cases in which I am working with more than one patient in a family (with parents and children or with husband and wife).

I insist on having the spouse, lover, or parent with whom the patient lives join us at least one time. This occurs at the beginning of therapy while we are deciding about working together. Almost all of the rest of the work is conducted with only myself and the patient present.

I do occasionally facilitate the introduction of a third party. The most obvious time for this occurs when, during the course of therapy, the patient moves in with a new lover or mate.

However, living together is not a necessary condition to my inviting in a third party. If the patient has a significant ongoing relationship which is troublesome, I point out the possibility of inviting the friend, roommate, boss, or relative to join us for at least one session. This offer is clearly defined to the patient as an *opportunity* rather than a demand. One other circumstance in which I would invite the entrance of a third party is when I have moved on into the middle phase of therapy with an adult patient whose aging parents live nearby, or are in town for a visit.

I bring up this possibility well in advance of any time when the patient might take advantage of it. It is introduced earlier as an invitation to a fantasy of what it would be like if that other person were here in the office with us.

This gives the patient a chance to work through some anxiety about the visit in advance. In any case, when we do discuss the more immediate possibility of having someone join us, some time must be taken to help the patient to accommodate to this possibility should it be chosen. Some patients immediately say: "That would be fine." Such a person is denying anxiety about the intrusion of the intimacy of our relationship. This may also be a way of avoiding facing the meaning of a revealing confrontation with the other person and whatever about it makes the patient uneasy.

Inviting such a patient to imagine what it would be like if mother (or whomever) should join us helps to get in touch with whatever might be dismaying about such an encounter, whatever is hoped or feared might happen. Either we work it through or we don't. I have no need for the other person to come in. My bringing it up with the patient is honestly no more than giving an opportunity to explore that aspect of life more directly.

If the patient doesn't choose to do so, that's fine with me. Most of the work in therapy has to do with getting into the feelings *within* the patient. Whether or not the politics of relationships with particular people gets worked out is up to the patient. The same inner problems would obtain even if the significant others were long dead.

The advance fantasy explorations involve the patient's imagining what it would be like to ask the other person to come, or insisting that the relative come if that is important to the patient. What would it be like if the other refused? What would it be like if the other accepted? Further, we can get into an active imagining of what would be the worst thing that could happen if the other party came, and what it would be like if it worked out in the best possible way.

One of the ways that I minimize any catastrophic implications that the patient may envision about such an encounter, is to say quite clearly: "If you decide to bring this person in to the therapy session, you needn't let me know in advance that you're going to do it. It's just a visit from that middle-aged lady (or gentleman) from Cleveland. I don't need to prepare in advance for our getting together."

Should the patient decide to bring in this third party, I warn that there will be a partial change in the confidentiality aspect of our contract. I tell the patient: "I will not needlessly reveal anything that you have told me in private when we get together with your husband (wife, parents, etc.). However, if when we are all together you tell him (or her, or them) one story when you have told me another then I may be in a different position. If your doing this leaves me in a helpless posture from which I cannot do my best work as a therapist with the two of you, then I will blow the whistle on you. I want you to know this in advance. If this is not acceptable to you, then it is best that we not work together in joint sessions at all."

If we do have a joint session it begins with the patient introducing me to the relative or friend. I remain silent for a minute or so, giving them a chance to begin wherever they like if they choose to. If nothing occurs spontaneously, I structure the situation. I do this in part because I know that the patient's anxiety is likely to be quite high, and also because the visitor has no contract with me as a patient. I must respect the visitor as a person in his or her own right (rather than as some appendage to the therapy of the patient). I must not presume that I am going to be accepted as this other person's therapist, even for an hour.

When visitors come in from out of town, if possible I arrange for the patient to bring them in for a session at a time when I have the following hour free. The contract is structured so that the patient pays for the time as if it were an individual hour. It is set up as one hour with an option for us to go on to a second hour only if we all choose to do so.

Let's say a male patient brings in his mother. If I need to structure the situation I do so by welcoming the visitor, letting her know that it's fine with me that she has come. Next I ask the visitor: "How do you understand your being invited to come here today? I'd like you to tell me what you were told about coming here, and what you expect. Then I will tell you where I stand in this matter. We'll see if we can agree as to what this is all about."

The visitor may say: "Well, he just asked me to come so I did," or "He said it would be a chance for us to work out some of the problems we have in getting along," or "He talks so much about you, I wanted a chance to meet you," etc.

I then go on to explain my view of the invitation: "You and he are very important to one another. I suggested that he invite you to come in because I believe meeting you will allow me to understand him better. That will help me in my work with him. (And where it applies) I understand that you two have some difficulty in getting along as well as you would like. If I can help to make things *clearer* between the two of you, I'll be glad to do that. Now I would like the two of you to help me to get to know something more about what it's like for you to be together. What can either one of you tell me about how it feels to have the other person in your life?"

The Work then ranges from people complaining about one another to their sharing warm, loving feelings. The patient may be inclined to present a bill of particulars about past disappointments, especially if the visitor is a parent. I tend to discourage rehashing an uncorrectable past. Instead I direct their attention to what it's like between them *now*.

The parent is sometimes defensive, assuming that she has been brought in to be blamed for the patient's unhappiness. I try to let her off the hook by shifting attention to my interest in getting to know her. It is especailly helpful if I can get her talking about her own parents and childhood. It is a singularly illuminating experience for a patient to have what is sometimes the first encounter with a parent as another human being (one who has disappointing parents of her own).

Sometimes these people say harsh things to each other which they have never said before. I operate at that point to make sure that they do not fall prey to the *psychoanalytic fallacy* of believing that whatever is negative, unconscious, or long unsaid is the *real* truth about the relationship. I insist on keeping their eyes open to the fact that any negative expression that comes up is no more than a piece of the overall relationship. If they did not matter to each other, we would not all be sitting there that day.

Feelings are often intense and surprises are not unusual. Sometimes the most traumatic experience for the patient is simply that even with my help, absolutely nothing can be done to change the relationship. The individual sessions that follow that kind of experience are usually deep immersion in helplessness and grief. Often this results in the freedom that comes from giving up attachment to the hope that things can be any different with that person.

These joint experiences are so singular that I cannot easily offer a set of expectations to the therapist who has not yet tried this arrangement. Perhaps the most important advice to offer is that the therapist limit the fantasy that he or she can *make* anything important come about in just an hour. I still occasionally get stuck with that one myself. I will offer just two examples to suggest the range of possibilities.

In the first instance I was treating a young man who was depressed about the ways in which he restricted his relationships. His feeling the need for the illusion of control in whatever he did was a burden.

He was an overt homosexual, but this was *not* a problem for him. He had come to trust me enough to understand that I was not going to change his life as a homosexual except to help to make it happier. He had become clearer about the ways in which he was both politically and personally intimidated by having to maintain a partially-hidden gay identity.

He had a single rewarding relationship in his family, with a younger sister. However, even this relationship was monumentally restricted by the fact that he was too fearful of rejection to have ever let her know that he was gay. During the course of therapy I had explored with him the fantasy of bringing in other people to a session. Later on, when his sister was visiting Washington, it was *his* idea to bring her in. He wanted to tell her that he was gay. He was not sure whether or not he had the courage to go through with it. We agreed that he would have her come into the session without his being committed to exposure during that hour.

His sister came along with him one morning. She turned out to be a very substantial human being, open about her feelings but scared of being found wanting in that situation. Early on in the session the patient chose to tell her: "There's something about me that you don't know. I'm very scared to tell you, but there's no way that we can be really close unless I do. What I want you to know is that I'm a homosexual."

His sister's response was to leap from her chair to embrace him. She cried and cried because she was touched so deeply that he would trust her with this. As they embraced she sobbed: "I love you, I've always loved you. I don't care what you are. I'm so grateful that you trust me enough to tell me." They cried and held each other for a long while before we went on to talk about it. I was tearful too, and grateful for their letting me be a part of this touchingly powerful meeting. My work during the session involved little more than helping them to deepen and clarify what they were going through together.

An experience at the other end of the scale occurs to me. It was a time when a married female patient in her thirties invited her aging mother to the session. It was during a holiday visit with the patient, the mother having traveled from her home in another part of the country.

The patient had been struggling in therapy to get beyond taking care of other people so that she could begin to take better care of herself. At the outset, expressing anger was difficult for her. She only gradually had begun to be able to complain when she felt other people were treating her badly. She saw this as a chance to straighten things out with her mother.

Bitterly she began by saying: "Momma, there's something I have to get straight with you. I'm trying to live a life of my own. I can't go on worrying about you and taking care of you. I'm not your good little girl any more. You're just going to have to take care of yourself. Calling you regularly and visiting you and taking care of things for you is just too much for me. I would like just to be able to call when I feel like it and not have to be *your* mother."

Momma listened intently, her expression shifting from hurt to resentment to some kind of devilish glee. When the patient finished, Momma took her on.

She spoke slowly and deliberately: "Look here. That's all in

your head. I haven't asked you to do any of those things for me
for a *long,* long time. It's true that when you were younger I
asked a lot from you. Things were hard and Poppa was always
so distant. But that was long ago. Now you and your sister have
been out of the house for a while. And since Poppa died two
years ago I've gotten my first job and I love it. I've got time
for myself to do the things I want to do. I even have a gentleman
friend. I don't need you to call me. Oh, I like talking to you
once in a while but I really can't be bothered with having my
children follow me around now that they're both grown. You don't
take care of me because *I* need it. You take care of me because
you need it."

The patient couldn't believe what she was hearing. But God
bless them, they worked it out. After some crying and some laughing,
they agreed to be grown-up friends. I was certain that they would
get back into their old stuff from time to time but it really sounded
like a new ball game.

Another aspect of changed parameters which need to be examined
is that of touching the patient. In earlier days when psychoanalytic
orientation dominated the field of psychotherapy, therapists never
touched patients. In recent years, during the upsurge of human
potential movement and humanistic psychotherapy, more and more
therapists engage in certain limited physical contact with patients.

I will *not* touch a patient unless we *both* are comfortable with
that aspect of the relationship. Like any other aspect of the
relationship, physical contact is never entered into an exploitive
manner, but rather only in the service of the therapeutic goals.

Touching has powerful immediacy as an experience and a
profound primitive quality that bypasses verbal defenses. Therefore
I never enter into this on a purely technical basis without genuine
feelings of wishing to participate in this intimacy with a patient.

I may take the patient's hand as a way of comforting, hold
a crying patient, or express closeness of a given moment by hugging.
Just as with any other change of parameter of the Work, touching
needs to be explored and analyzed afterward. Callous and unfeeling
as that may sound, not doing that technical part of the work serves
only to invite the patient to join me in a potentially destructive
misalliance. In the absence of exploration and analysis of the
meaning of what is going on between us, changes in the parameters

of therapy merely serve to sacrifice the Work to the living out of a mutual fantasy in which we each promise to be more to the other than will ever be delivered.

CHANGES INTRODUCED BY THE PATIENT

Some changes are introduced by the patient rather than by the therapist. The therapist need not comply. For example, the patient may suggest physical contact by asking to be held. I *must* choose to refuse if that does not feel right to me. I do not trust the genuineness of the therapist who says "yes" to such requests, without also feeling free to say "no."

I only introduce changes in parameters of the therapeutic relationship on those rare occasions when there is particularly good reason to do so. Even then their impact must be explored with the patient in ways that follow the guidelines of careful practice.

Frequently it is the patient who instigates the changes, usually as *requests*. Such matters are often introduced very casually in the form of business or social transactions about which no serious discussion or analysis is expected. Those changes presented as if they were no more than administrative or business matters usually are brought up at the very beginning or at the very end of the hour. In the first case the patient may introduce the matter with the statement: "Before we begin I would like to ask . . ." In the second instance, on the way out: "Oh, there's something I wanted to ask you about but I didn't want to interrupt the therapy session with it."

Those changes which the patient is likely to present as if they were not really a part of the therapeutic process include: third party payments (by insurance companies or parents), arrangements for changing the contract about time (rescheduling of appointments, vacations, time off, increasing or decreasing frequency of sessions, etc.), altering financial arrangements (requests for permission to delay payment, for reduced fees, etc.)

There is a second category of changes in the parameters that the patient defines as other than part of the process and therefore not subject to therapeutic scrutiny. These transactions are considered by the patient to be merely "social." They include: asking the therapist for a cigarette or for a match, or offering one, asking what time it is, asking to borrow a book or a waiting-room magazine, asking the therapist to repeat something just said, etc.

A third category of requests for change of parameter that the patient may not expect to require exploration includes intra-session matters of arrangements and therapist participation. Examples in this category include: asking to sit somewhere else, asking the therapist to sit closer, talk more, give information, advice, etc., and asking the therapist questions about his or her personal life.

It is crucial to the Work that none of these requests go by unexamined. They are all grist for the therapeutic mill. The patient will often protest: "You shrinks are so paranoid. You think everything has something hidden behind it, some deep unconscious meaning." or "You don't trust me. Why can't you ever just take me at my word?" or "You're so callous, so detached, so goddamned professional. If you really liked me you'd be willing to do me a favor once in a while without insisting that we analyze it."

> Of course, whatever the unceremonial nature of psychotherapy, patient and therapist are real people, operating within a culturally sanctioned social context, fulfilling an economic contract. Their basic *therapeutic alliance* involves an agreement to work together at a specified time and place, their mutual task being to help the patient to be happier. The therapist is a professional who exchanges expert services for money, the patient a client who pays for help.
>
> But . . . [in addition to] the therapeutic alliance . . . [there is also] the *therapeutic barrier.* This transforming barrier is the therapist's prerogative to act at any point *as if* the situation were not real. The patient and I meet as any two free agents might, talking his problems out *between* us. But at any time I may shift the focus onto the *way* in which he is discussing the matter, saying, "You react as if I were your father (or your mother, brother, etc.).[3]

The patient may attempt to define any piece of behavior as just business or only social. No matter. For the therapist, nothing that goes on between them lies outside of the therapeutic context. Each attempt by the patient to change the boundaries of the therapeutic arrangement needs to be analyzed. When the patient makes any move toward changing the ways in which they have contracted to be together, the therapist's first intervention is that of *silence.*

The patient asks me for a match to light a cigarette, for a change of appointment, or for a piece of advice. I invite the patient's attention to whatever might underlie this request by delaying any verbal response just a bit longer than one might in ordinary conversation. Because transactions of this sort occur again and again in therapy, the patient soon comes to learn that my posture implies that anything the patient says or does is open to scrutiny and to interpretation. Most patients quickly begin to take responsibility for analyzing their own requests for change.

After the first few transactions with a therapist who consistently makes sure to invite careful attention to any new piece of behavior, the patient will often initiate exploration of the underlying meaning of any attempts to change the relationship. If the anxiety is not too high, the patient may then respond to my silence by saying: "Oh, I suppose it would be useful to me to try to understand why I want you to do this for me today."

If not, I may then indicate that any decision on the matter is to be set aside for the moment in favor of exploring what might underly the request. One simple way to do this is to say to the patient: "This sounds like something that might be useful for us to talk about. How do you understand your bringing up this matter at just this time?"

Any exploration of the patient's behavior is in service of heightening self-awareness, of deepening self-understanding. When enough of the background data becomes available, it is often possible to make a useful interpretation.

I have telescoped the example I am about to give. The actual movement from request to interpretation took longer. The path was more erratic. The Work was less competent. Still this example offers the essence of such transactions.

The patient, a bright young professional working as a member of the administrative staff of a social agency, had talked the week before (in his sixth session) about how little attention he had gotten from his father while he was growing up. He treasured those few instances when the old man had taken the trouble to spend time alone with him.

But even these memories were bitter-sweet. They were restricted to times when the father had seen him as too dumb to do something on his own. He might then be persuaded to help the son to learn some simple skill such as the putting up of a screen door. How well he remembered father's sighs of exasperation as he labored through showing his witless son how to perform some simple chore. Still, for the patient it was better than being ignored.

The next session, the patient came in with a sheaf of papers in his hand. Leaning forward in his chair, he held out the papers to me, saying:

P: "Before we begin today, I'd like to take care of a business matter. I need you to help me fill out these health insurance forms."

T: (Silence.) (Does not accept the proferred papers.)

P: "I've just gotten this insurance coverage. This is the first time I've had to make out a claim form. It's probably not all that hard except that it's all new for me."

T: (Silence.)

P: "You've probably signed hundreds of these forms. I guess it must seem dumb to you that I don't know how to make one out."

T: "You sound as though this is uncomfortable for you. Maybe there's more to it than just a 'business matter'."

P: "Well, it *is* your responsibility to take care of this. I don't know how to do it. I just wanted to get it out of the way today before we begin to talk about my problems."

T: "We *have* begun to talk about one of your problems."

P: "Oh, you mean my complaining about how incompetent I feel sometimes? You're right. I guess I should know how to fill out a form. It's a big part of what I do for a living."

T: "Sometimes you feel incompetent about doing tasks you've done many times before. A couple of sessions ago, you told me that happens at work most often when your boss is around."

P: "Yeah. I guess he makes me nervous. It seems like the only time he has something to say to me is when he thinks I'm fucking up."

T: "If you knew how to put up a screen door all by yourself, he'd never pay any attention to you."

P: "A screen door . . . What's that got to do with . . . ? Oh, you mean like what I was telling you last time about my father.

(His facial expression saddens and his voice begins to quaver, but he restrains his tears.)

T: "It hurts so much for a kid to feel that the only time his old man pays any attention to him is when he's fucking up."

P: (Begins to sob.) "Yeah. Most of the time he acted like I wasn't even around. He was always too busy to take time out for me. Too busy except when he could show me how smart he was by letting me know how dumb I was."

T: "But what can a kid do? He has to settle for what he can get."

P: (More sobbing.) "You think that's why I'm still a fuck-up."

T: "I think that's why you still have trouble expecting that anyone whom you look up to would be willing to spend time with you unless you gave him something to criticize. Without realizing it you end up degrading yourself again and again by acting as if you need help on some trivial task that you could really do yourself. It's just so hard for you to imagine that someone whom you would have liked to have as a father would be interested in spending time with you just to get to know you."

P: (A smile breaks through his tears.) "I guess I can really make out these insurance forms myself. I'll just bring them back next time for your signature. Maybe it can be different here with you than it was at home. Who knows? I may even be putting stuff off on my boss that really belongs to my father."

Such a resolution is not unusual. Often exploration of the underlying meaning of the patient's request for a change results in my not having to decide whether to say "yes" or "no." A patient who is not too anxious may respond to a correct interpretation by accepting increased awareness of what the request is really about. At that point the initial surface behavior is transformed into nothing more than a signpost indicating that something else is going on, something old and emotionally important. Once the underlying tension is shifted back to its origin, the patient may become curious about what it all means. Usually there is no further need to insist that the derivative request be met.

Even those requests that are grounded in realistic need may

carry additional meanings. For example, the health insurance company may require that each month's claim be accompanied by a form signed by the therapist. After the first such transaction, it would be deadly to re-explore this with the patient again and again each month.

The therapist and the patient have agreed that one will bring the form and the other will sign it. Once this is free of unanalyzed transference, the patient can carry out his or her part on an adult-to-adult basis. I can fulfill my own commitment to sign the form without further comment *unless* some new aspect of the patient's behavior suggests that some part of the transaction is once again in the service of a hidden agenda. Examples of this might include the patient's commenting: "Today I feel nervous about asking you to sign this" or "It's really nice of you to sign these forms for me" or something of the sort. The communication may be non-verbal, such as an irritable tossing of the form onto my desk or an unusual hesitancy in handing it to me. When such behavior accompanies the agreed-upon transaction, I am once again required to raise the therapeutic barrier. I do this by commenting on the behavior in a way that invites the patient's attention to the meaning of these elaborations.

Initial requests can be met with structuring that turns the patient's attention toward any unconscious fantasies within which the request may be embedded. For example:

P: (The patient takes out a cigarette.) "May I have a light?"

T: (Silence.) (Does not offer a light.)

P: "I asked if I could have a light."

T: "What would it be like for you if I lit your cigarette?"

P: "No big deal. That's just the sort of thing people ordinarily do for each other."

T: "How would it be if I said 'no'?"

P: "That would feel awful. It would make me mad. (Silence. Patient is obviously remembering something.) I was thinking last night that you're never considerate and polite. I'm just a customer to you. You only see me because I pay you. I don't believe you really care about me at all."

At this point the therapist is in a position to make a preliminary interpretation that invites further exploration by the patient.

The patient's introduction of a change in the therapeutic contract need *not* always be expressed in the form of an explicit request. Instead wishes may be acted out without being discussed. In that case the therapist is presented with a change in the form of an accomplished fact. Examples of such imposed changes in the relationship by the patient include: telephone calls and letters to the therapist, entering the office before the appointed time of a session or staying beyond the hour, delaying payment beyond the due date, bringing gifts to the therapist, bringing food and drink into the office, taking handfuls of the therapist's Kleenex home, coming to the session high on alcohol or dope, and precipitous termination.

The therapist must avoid reinforcing the patient's acting-out. I do this by withholding the expected social response. In order to carry this off, I must be willing to tolerate the patient's hurt and angry response to what is likely to be seen as my arbitrary, unreasonable, rude, uncaring, even hateful behavior.

The probability that the patient may become aware of the hidden feelings beneath the demands is entirely dependent on my disengagement. I may be tempted to allow the acting-out by ignoring it, thus unwittingly giving tacit approval. I may criticize the acting-out, and put myself in the position of the restricting parent, or I may be tempted to *explain* to the patient why this is not beneficial. In that case I make the mistake of taking protective responsibility for a piece of the patient's life.

Instead, what is called for is an interruption of the transaction, and if need be, a non-punitive confrontation. For example, when the patient does not pay on time, I begin the session that follows by saying: "It's my impression that I have not received your check this month." Because I am capable of an occasional clerical error, I do *not* simply announce that the bill has not been paid.

If the patient phones me, I listen only long enough to determine if the call has been made to cancel an appointment. If the intent is to talk about anything else, I interrupt quickly saying: "We can talk about that during your next session." When we do meet, if the patient does not bring up the call, *I* do. There may be an attempt to restrict the discussion to the patient's depression.

I insist on focusing on the fact that this depression was dealt with by phoning me. This may well get us into an exploration of the need for me to take care of the patient, of hurt and anger that I didn't, etc.

If I receive a letter from the patient, I need not read it. Should the patient overstay the hour, I need not remain in the office. I know one therapist who left, came back ten minutes later to begin his next hour and found the first patient still seated in the office. The therapist simply went about his business by bringing in his next patient from the waiting-room. The first patient left in embarrassment. The matter was explored when he returned the following week for his next scheduled appointment.

Sometimes patients bring in written materials such as parts of journals, notes about a dream they had, letters from relatives, and the like. Should the patient expect me to read these during the hour, it is sometimes enough to point out that if he or she wants me to know what the writings are about, they can be read aloud by the patient. This is the only way that the full emotional charge of the communication will come across. The repeated bringing in of written materials must also be analyzed in the service of exploring the possibility that they are being used to avoid the patient's presenting the material in a less controlled way. The writings may act to block other spontaneous productions. They may also be offered as polished productions which the patient feels will be more acceptable than spontaneous talking.

The patient may bring in or mail in written materials asking me to read them *between* sessions. This burdensome demand is a request for special treatment that the patient often fantasizes as keeping me thinking about our relationship when we are not together. Early in my work I agreed to do this if the patient paid me for my time. This was an error. Paying for such treatment did not make it any less special for the patient. It still constituted our acting out an unexamined fantasy (such as making up for not being given enough attention as a child).

Dealing with a patient who changes the parameters of therapy by coming to the session high on alcohol or dope can be a complex matter. The extent of intoxication may either be exaggerated or minimized by the patient. The therapist cannot decide just how high the patient *really* is.

Coming in high is fraught with fantasies. These include the testing of limits by the patient to see how much acting out I will allow, the wish to be less inhibited in communication with me, an attempt to be in a less responsible position for what is done in the hour, the testing out of my attitude toward self-indulgence, etc.

It is often difficult to explore the meaning of this behavior at the time simply because the patient's focus of attention may be distorted and the dialogue may later be forgotten.

My inclination is to begin exploration with the patient there and then. If it is a grass high this will usually bring the patient down enough to do the work (if not too stoned to begin with). If the patient is not available for such work, I hold it off for the next session. I am not willing to spend an entire session with a patient who is too high to participate in therapeutic dialogue, any more than I would be willing to have a serious talk with a friend who was very drunk.

If we don't get anywhere together in the first ten or fifteen minutes of such a session, I ask the patient to leave. I point out that though I cannot be sure just how high he or she is, I can be sure that we can't work together this way. In this case, both the coming in high and my putting the patient out will have to be explored in the course of the next session.

There are times when a patient may request time off from therapy. This may be done directly by expressing a wish to be "on my own for a while" or because of financial difficulties, family vacation plans, the need to enter the hospital for surgery, etc. Each of these must be explored for underlying meanings such as avoidance of upsetting materials, testing of limits, limiting closeness with the therapist, fear of dependency, etc.

Some traditional therapists believe that the patient's taking time off is so unalterably disruptive to the Work that they will not go on working with a patient who insists on interrupting in this way. (Some hold the same position with regard to the patient engaging in additional therapeutic activities such as encounter groups and the like).

My practice is first to begin by exploring the meaning of the patient's wish to take time off. *I neither give nor withhold permission.* I do make it clear that our contract calls for paying for missed appointments. If the decision calls for being away for more than a month, I insist that we terminate our present contract.

The patient may bring up the matter of resuming our contract when he or she is ready to return. I *never* guarantee that I will resume work with a patient in the future. The patient is free to call me. *If* it feels right to me then, I will offer another appointment *when* I have time open.

A young therapist learns most easily to carefully explore those patient-introduced changes that are experienced as negative demands. The therapist's own discomfort serves as immediate motivation. The analysis of seemingly neutral or irrelevant minor changes requires more task-oriented discipline on the part of the therapist. Changes that make the therapist feel good are the most difficult ones on which to focus clearly the impeccable work that is required.

In this way, such changes pose the same problems as presented in the analyzing of transference reactions. How much easier it is for the young therapist to see the necessity of exploring the patient's criticism and hatred than to see the need to question the patient's admiration and love. Often the young therapist is more likely to question late payments, than the checks received from the patient who consistently pays the bill *immediately* after receiving it.

The patient who misses sessions or comes late is called to task. The one who lets the therapist know about regularly coming early to spend half an hour in the waiting room is smiled upon.

So too, a patient who asks to come to therapy less often is more likely to be challenged than a patient who asks to increase the frequency of treatment from one session to two sessions a week. In the service of the therapeutic process, it is just as important to explore the meaning of a request to increase frequency as to question the patient's wish to decrease our hours.

Gifts constitute another clear instance of patient-induced change that many therapists feel inhibited about challenging. Conventional wisdom understands a gift as an act of friendliness with the expectation that the receiver will be grateful. So great is this expectation that any questioning of a gift is likely to arouse painful, embarrassed feelings.

It is helpful for the therapist to remain focused on the fact that gifts are usually objects of exchange implying a wish to maintain control of a social balance. Certainly there are times when gifts between people in personal situations are simple expressions of affection, offered freely out of abundance, without demand for a return gift. In therapy they are to be questioned just as any other patient-introduced change in the relationship is subject to scrutiny.

In my own practice there are two instances in which I would hold off examination of the transaction until *after* it occurred. These exceptions involve receiving small token gifts from very young patients (children and early adolescents) and from debilitated psychotic patients.

The problem in dealing with gifts from patients is further complicated in that they need not come in the obvious form of wrapped, beribboned presents. Gifts from patients may include reporting of progress, valued productions (such as dreams or early childhood recollections), invitations, and useful information (stock market tips, recommended readings, etc.).

A patient may arrive with a traditional wrapped gift that is handed to the therapist on entering the office. At that point I may simply put the gift down on the floor between our chairs or on the table beside me and remain silent. Simply withholding the expected deferential gesture of saying: "Thank you" and *not* opening the gift is usually enough to bring the patient's attention to the exploration of the transaction. Hurt and angry feelings usually ensue.

One patient began by telling me that she had brought me flowers because she loved me. Her response to my not accepting them was a flood of previously-hidden murderous rage that the gift was meant to disguise. In other instances, the major focus is the patient's wish to please me. This usually implies deep feelings of unworthiness for which the gift is meant to compensate.

The patient need not offer me any more than has been agreed upon in contracting to be a patient. In turn I myself give enough when I offer impeccable work. This does *not* include complying with the patient's demands. It is required only that I assume the Karma Yoga posture of doing my job with the devotion of giving myself to it as fully as I can by concentrating on the Work itself, rather than on the fruits of my labor.

In the absence of attachment to results, the therapist creates an atmosphere of acceptance within which the patient can increase understanding of his or her own behavior, of Self, and way of living. As the therapist, my role is that of the non-judgmental, attentive listener who speaks only when I have something useful to say.

After all, I am *only a psychotherapist!* The practice of Karma Yoga is no different for a psychotherapist than it is for a tailor or for a shoemaker. Each can offer the work as an act of devotion. For each, every action of daily life can be an act of love. "Washing dishes with love is yoga."[4]

The value of what is offered depends on its being given freely, out of the highest consciousness the therapist can attain and without attachment to results. The excellence of the Work depends on the therapist's clarity of concentration on any particular technique that is being practiced. Every proposed change in the relationship must be approached and analyzed with this in mind.

Chapter 7

Impasses

The therapeutic impasse is a needless power struggle between patient and therapist. Most often it begins with the therapist trying to pressure the patient into doing something that he or she is not ready to do. When the therapist's part in this struggle is recognized, it can get unstuck by going *back to one*. This is accomplished by the therapist returning the focus to the basic therapeutic intervention that is called for at that point.

There is a second kind of impasse that begins with repeated behavior by the patient that limits or interrupts the Therapeutic Process. Such characteristic defensive patterns include both conscious and unconscious defection from the process by "symptomatic" lateness, absence, or distraction of the patient's attention away from inner experience. Such patient-induced impasses do *not* yield readily to the usual basic therapeutic interventions.

As a result the therapist often feels frustrated in efforts to promote the Therapeutic Process. The therapist's sense of helplessness in trying to get beyond these "resistances" often leads to unwarranted blaming of the patient, to stubborn pushing against the defenses, and to both giving up in despair.

The patient's defensive avoidances are old ways of behaving, maintained by continuing reinforcement. Like all avoidant behaviors, these escapist tactics must be repeated lest something terrible happen. Each time the patient does *not* face something, the dreaded catastrophe does *not* occur! Again and again the seeming wisdom of avoidance is negatively confirmed.

Originally, these avoidances were developed as techniques for emotional survival. They served to save the patient from the overwhelming anxiety of being fully aware of unbearable childhood situations. Though the original danger is long past, any pressure by the therapist to get the patient to give up these old defenses simply increases the "resistance."

In the context of the therapeutic relationship, the struggle between

103

awareness and avoidance begins as an internal conflict within the patient. The therapist's pushing for greater awareness increases the patient's anxiety and strengthens the defenses against it. What began as the patient's personal problem becomes an interpersonal impasse between patient and therapist.

Participation in the Therapeutic Process requires that the patient give up certain distractions from deeper consciousness. Comparable problems arise in the practice of Yoga. The aspirant must make certain painful sacrifices in the interest of pursuing spiritual liberation.

Religious rules of conduct have been developed that require the Yogi to transcend the distractions of the flesh. It is as difficult for the psychotherapy patient to give up the comforts of distracting "resistances" as it is for the Yogi to overcome these temptations. In either case, should the guru push the aspirant to get on with it, a power struggle ensues in which the distracting behaviors are likely to increase.

In the practice of Yoga there is a "left-handed" approach to transcending this problem. It is called *Tantra*. It works by transforming the distractions into new ways of attaining spiritual awareness. The previously forbidden acts of eating, drinking, and sexual practices now become the sacramental fare of Tantric rites.

The guru guides the devotee in participating in the forbidden acts. Once transformed, they are no longer acts of attachment to the flesh. Paradoxically, carried out in a controlled state of consciousness, they become acts of devotion in the service of spiritual illumination.

The psychotherapist can bring this same spirit of sacred carnival to meeting the patient-induced impasses. The psychotherapeutic technique that parallels *Tantra* is called *Paradox*. Like *Tantra*, Paradox transforms "resistances" into the very consciousness from which they previously served to distract.

The therapist uses Paradox as a way of accepting the patient's avoidant behavior and then redefining it. The patient is instructed to continue to do what he or she is already doing. Going along with the therapist's instructions means participating in the therapeutic alliance. "Resisting" the instructions requires giving up the counter-therapeutic behavior. In any case, paradox redefines the meaning of the patient's behavior so that the avoidances themselves become a form of patient-participation.

> The emphasis . . . [in Paradox] is not on the struggle to control another person, but rather on the struggle to control the *definition* of a relationship.[1]

There are three basic paradoxical instructions:
(1) "Continue to do exactly what you are doing."
(2) "Do even more of what you are already doing."
(3) "Know that what you are doing means the exact opposite of what you believe it means."

I used the first type of paradoxical instruction with a patient who repeatedly became completely distracted. Whenever we began to speak about his relationship with his mother his focus of attention shifted. At such times, all he was aware of was the sounds of birds singing outside the office window, of trash removal trucks in the parking lot, and of the distant sirens of passing emergency vehicles.

He accepted my interpretation that this was his way of avoiding his anxiety about his relationship with his mother. Unfortunately, he insisted, there was nothing he could do about it. I agreed, and suggested that it was crucial that he continue to do this *for a while.*

My paradoxical instructions were: "Any time the topic of your mother comes up, you are to immediately pay complete attention to whatever sounds you can hear coming from outside the office window. Whenever this happens, you will know 'This is the way that I can avoid thinking about Mother.'"

The exaggeration demanded by the second type of paradoxical instruction is best suited to *measurable* avoidant behaviors, such as chronic lateness. It proved useful with a man I had been seeing for several weeks who came *exactly* ten minutes late to *every* session. When I pointed this out he admitted feeling upset about this *uncontrollable* behavior. It turned out that he was always ten minutes late, no matter what kind of appointment he had.

Though precise in his imprecision, this master of *un*punctuality experienced himself as helpless to do anything about this pattern.

He understood that it cost him one fifth of his therapy time but could take no responsibility for what he was doing. As with all neurotic symptoms, he was able to come late without feeling that he chose to do so.

I told him that if he instructed me to do so, I would arrange for him to cure himself of this symptom. He was hesitantly enthusiastic about the prospect. I suggested that for our next session he plan to come *fifteen* minutes late, rather than ten.

He balked at the idea of wasting five minutes. I assured him that by risking these five minutes he might eventually be able to save the time that his "symptom" of chronic lateness usually wasted.

The next session he arrived fifteen minutes late, and absolutely furious. He said that he could not stand the idea of his having had to *wait for me* those last five minutes. In response to this transaction, he soon gave up coming late. The paradoxical experience also contributed to his growing recognition of the secret hostile power that he unconsciously fantasized wielding over those who waited for him.

The third type of paradoxical instruction involves redefining the meaning of the avoidant behavior. This served well with one young woman whom I once treated. She was very frightened by any experience of personal intimacy. Any such closeness was followed by the demand for equal time to be given over to withdrawal. The first few weeks of our working together were characterized by dramatic alternations of contact and distancing.

In any given session, she might feel safe enough to be personally revealing. At those times she was able to increase her self-awareness by temporarily tolerating being vulnerable to my getting to know her. Invariably, in our next meeting she could only chat superficially about circumstantial matters. Her inner feelings were never revealed either to me or to herself during those intervening sessions.

Despite my pointing out and interpreting her avoidant behavior, this predictable interruption of the Therapeutic Process went on regularly for many weeks. We met twice a week, but it was as though she was in therapy only half the time.

My use of basic interventions resulted in her being *more* distant. As protection against my coercive confrontations, after any contact session she was even more out of touch with herself. Clearly, a shift to the paradoxical mode was needed.

The next time she began to behave in her defensively distancing manner, I said to her: "You are pulling back from me and from yourself again. It's very important that you feel free to chat about superficial things at times like this. Whenever you do, I will understand that during our last meeting you felt so close to me and so in touch with yourself, that you must run from that today. I like the fact that you never have to stay any closer than you can bear."

Later I added elaborations of the paradox by telling her, "It's very important that you be able to hide out after any session in which you have come to know more about yourself. Whenever you do this I will understand that you are telling me that you feel very close to me and that you are on the threshold of learning even more about yourself. It is so frightening for you to become more aware of what is going on that *for a while* your telling me how close you feel will be limited to shifting into your chatty pose."

Her first response to what I said was a denial. But along with it came a smile of confirmation. Soon she began to acknowledge to herself that her chatting must mean that she still felt open to what had gone on between us in the previous session. Gradually this alternation between vulnerability and self-protection narrowed into shifts of behavior within a given session. Eventually the times of withdrawal were restricted to a few chatty moments of assuring herself that she could draw back when she needed to.

When not transcended by Paradox, the seemingly minor patient-induced impasses can be deadly to the Therapeutic Process. Unfortunately they usually receive less attention than the more dramatic interruptive impasse involving the promise of sex or the threat of violence.

In the first type of impasse the process is undone by lateness, absence, and distraction. In the other it comes to a standstill as concentration centers on the dramatic issues of romance or mayhem. Whether ridiculous or sublime, each type of impasse is maintained by the therapist's attachment to getting his or her own way.

When psychotherapist and patient meet, both positive and negative attachments can evoke therapeutic impasses. The impact of the compelling attraction to *sexuality* and of the fearful withdrawal

from *violence* offer two clear examples. Each leads the therapist
to care what the patient does in a way that puts pressure on the
patient to behave (or not to behave) in some particular way.

An impasse to the Therapeutic Process arises out of the power
struggle that ensues. Resolution depends on the proper shift in
the therapist's attention. By going *back to one*, it is possible to
get unstuck. In giving up *one* side of the power struggle, the
therapist presents the patient with an opportunity for similar
self-liberation.

As a male therapist, my own experiences of getting stuck in
sexual impasses are restricted to flawed work with heterosexual
female, and homosexual male patients. I assume that parallel
experiences occur for female therapists working with heterosexual
male, and homosexual female patients. It would be instructive
to read accounts of how such impasses and resolutions differ from
my own.

The sexual longings that arise between patient and therapist
may be viewed as expressions of transference and counter-transference. If so, they require careful therapeutic analysis. Instead,
these desires may be understood as predictable, natural erotic
responses of two people who like each other and have the opportunity to spend extended time alone together. Viewed from that
perspective, the matter requires no further analysis.

In either case, the acting out of explicit sexuality between patient
and therapist is *always* counter-therapeutic. It parallels the confusing double-roles of an incestuous family. In a therapeutic relationship, sex might be good fun, but it is always bad politics.

Albert Ellis is one of the therapists who view most sexual longings
between patient and therapist as the normal biosocial desires that
would occur:

> if the same participants encountered each other for any length of
> time in a non-therapy relationship . . .[2]

Even so, he sees great *dis*advantages in a male therapist having
intercourse with a female patient.

> [He] may well prove to be a disappointing sex-love partner to her.
> He will probably end the affair within a fairly short period of

time—especially if he is having sex relations with several of his other patients, too! He is likely to be sexually rather than amatively attracted to his patient, while she is likely to be much more emotionally involved with him. He may well be consciously or unconsciously exploiting her sexually. He will often encourage her to be dishonest with him, as a patient, because she is interested in continuing with their sex-love relationship. He may be sorely tempted to gratify her sick needs for being loved, and make her unusually dependent on him rather than help her to become truly independent in her own right. He will tend to leave her without a suitable therapist if their sex affair ends. He will lose objectivity in diagnosing and treating her. . . .

Legally he may be convicted of statuatory rape, especially if he induces the patient to have sex relations with him in order to help her treatment. Professionally, he is engaging in unethical behavior and may well be dismissed from the reputable societies of which he is a member. He also gets in difficulties with his other patients, particularly with jealous females with whom he is *not* having any sex relations! . . . He may easily be blackmailed . . . and he may well draw down upon himself the wrath of a large segment of his community.[3]

As Ellis would acknowledge, there is more to the problem of dealing with sexuality in the therapy relationship than just these practical, rational considerations. For all of us, sex can be a ready arena in which a variety of willful struggles may be enacted. In any relationship, sexuality may serve other needs, such as dependency, power, or even hostility. The psychotherapeutic alliance is especially vulnerable to such distortions. In any case, the therapeutic goal of self-awareness demands that no experience of transaction go unexamined.

Some years ago, the psychoanalytic mode predominated. In that era, the young male therapist was often tempted to try to talk the patient out of her threateningly tempting sexual longings. By reducing these feelings to nothing more than "positive transference," he would attempt to interpret them away. This turned out to be an uneven contest.

. . . the hysteric makes sexuality out of the therapist's science, or the therapist makes science out of the sexuality. In this affair, the hysteric has the advantage, there being more sex to science than vice versa.[4]

During the sixties and seventies, Humanistic Psychotherapy began to come to the fore. With it came an emphasis on feeling, on experiencing things in the here and now, and on the therapeutic alliance as a beautiful encounter between two struggling human beings. The same problems continue to arise, but now they are understood by the therapist in a new way.

A young, attractive female patient may still tell her middle-aged male therapist that she is in love with him. Letting him know how wonderful he is, she will make it clear that she would like to go to bed with him. Too often, the Humanistic therapist can see her point.

He experiences her as truly appreciating how "together" he is. He forgets how often beautiful 20-year old women in therapists' offices have fallen madly in love with dull, bald, paunchy, 60-year old men. The phenomenon is called transference. *Any man* sitting in his therapist's chair would have seemed as engaging to a patient caught up in the flow of the Therapeutic Process.

The impasse that occurs in that process is not caused by the patient's sexuality but by the therapist's *attachment* to it. Feeling ethically bound *not* to have sex with the patient, he may still hedge about giving up his attachment to that wish. This can lead to his seeking the fantasy satisfaction that goes with a non-explicit sexual game.

He chooses *not* to have sex with the patient. Still he wants to experience the patient's attraction to him *as though* it was a personal response to his charm. He is careful not to be "rejecting" of the patient's "love," lest he hurt *her* feelings.

> Because feeling has been so blown up recently people have come to take it as the panacea for therapy.[5]

The outcome of such attachment games was clearly demonstrated in one of my supervisory seminar sessions. A therapist and his female patient had come to talk about *their* problems of her continuing insistence that they make love. He insisted that he had told her very clearly that they would not. It turned out that he had also let her know that he was sure that under other circumstances, their making love would have been a beautiful experience.

His only reason for refusing was that it would not be good *for her.* Professional responsibilities did not permit him such an untherapeutic indulgence. Despite his making all of this clear to her, he complained, she went on trying to convince him that he should change his mind.

I asked the patient what message she had been getting from her therapist. Her response was clear and perceptive: "When he says 'no' *that way,* I hear him telling me, 'not yet, we're still negotiating.'" The patient recognized that the therapist's attachment to his sexual longings was far more significant than all his talk about professional responsibility.

Much of this struggle could have been avoided. From the beginning, the patient's sexual overture could have been bracketed into the Therapeutic Process. In the absence of attachment, the therapist's concentration on the Work could have transformed the overture into further grist for the therapeutic mill. A therapeutic response was called for that communicated the message: "Your sexual *fantasy* about our relationship will give you the opportunity to learn more about yourself."

Most therapists understand at the outset that sexual attachment to patients is counter-therapeutic. Still, like young Augustine, they entreat: "Lord, grant me chastity and continency . . . but not yet."

Free of attachment, the therapist might have realized that, after all, it was *only* sex. This would allow his getting on with understanding enough to interpret the meaning of the sexual material in terms of the context in which it arose and of the associations that accompanied it. In this way, the exchange can turn out to be yet another way for the patient to become more aware of the underlying meaning of her behavior.

It is curiously degrading for a woman to offer sex to a man whom she hires as a therapist and to whom she already pays $50 an hour. Often it turns out that the patient feels that she does not have enough to offer as a person, or that she has hidden needs to control the therapist, to rob him of his power, to prove that she cannot depend on him, etc. Sacrificing awareness of these unconscious motives is very costly.

Even when the therapist *appears* to shift into an exclusively therapeutic interest in the patient's sexuality, another teasing impasse may ensue. "In the interests of the treatment," he may pressure the patient to turn him on with graphically-detailed descriptions of her fantasies.

This potential impasse can sometimes be avoided without loss to the patient. The therapist can suggest: "You have begun to see how costly it is for you to miss knowing any part of yourself. It will be easier for you to let yourself experience these sexual fantasies if you remember that there is no need for you to report them to me. As with anything that comes to mind, you may talk of them if *you* wish, and I will listen as I always do. But it is just as important that you understand that *I* have no need to know everything that you think or feel."

Later on in the therapeutic relationship, the patient and the therapist may develop simpler, more direct sexual feelings for one another. People who spend time together in an intimate setting often develop sexual, as well as other feelings of mutual attraction. Such feelings may be largely free of transference and counter-transference implications. If the therapist is concentrating on promoting the Therapeutic Process, there will be no attachment great enough to distract from doing the Work. The therapist who is not in touch with, and accepting of sexual longings will be especially vulnerable to enmeshing himself in sexual impasses.

A parallel problem arises around the potential threat of violence. The therapist is likely to be intimidated, uncertain, and inconsistent in response to a patient's hostility if not acceptingly aware of his or her own destructive anger. By knowing my own potential for self-protective rage, I need not avoid conflict with another in order to hide from myself that I might want to kill that person. Knowing my dark side and still valuing my own worth is my best protection against the impact of the patient's hatred.

However, there is a very real difference between sex and violence in the therapeutic context. The patient and I will *not* have sex unless I *willingly* participate. But I may be in danger of violent assault *in spite of* my wish to avoid it. Therefore, if I feel afraid that a patient will hurt me physically, I will *not* work with that patient. Though I have been menaced by psychiatric-ward patients whom I did not know, I have never been attacked by anyone with whom I was working.

One of the only two rules in my basic therapeutic contract is that the patient will do no violence to my person or to my property.

After all, I am *only* a psychotherapist. My commitment to my work does not call for subjecting myself to mortal danger.

Verbal expression of the patient's anger is always permissible. To the extent that I am comfortable with my own anger, I will not be threatened by the patient's hostile words. Depending on when and how it emerges, all that this hostility invites from me will be one of the basic therapeutic interventions (reflection of feelings, confrontation, structural questioning, silence, or interpretation).

There is one other exception. I am *not* willing to be an accomplice to violence committed by one person upon another. For example, when one patient told me that he was considering "taking out a contract" on his wife's life, I judged it to be part of a fantasy that he would *not* act upon. As such, I dealt with it as I would any other revelation of his inner self. Had I believed that there was serious chance that he might act on this fantasy, I would have taken the following position: "You are planning to have your wife murdered. I will *not* be a part of that. I am going to report this matter to the police and terminate my work with you."

Suicide is another matter entirely. I believe that everyone has a right to choose to end his or her own life.[6] I am personally responsive to the anguish that goes with feeling like killing oneself. I have been through it myself. To this despair, I respond compassionately. However, to threats and unsuccessful attempts at suicide, I respond with confrontation and interpretation of these behaviors as acting out to avoid underlying feelings of rage, helplessness, etc.

Aside from my contributions to the Therapeutic Process, I leave the decision up to the patient as to whether to end life or to go on with it. A patient may call me to tell me that he or she is feeling too bad to make it through the weekend without committing suicide. I respond by pointing out: "If you feel you cannot make it through the weekend without killing yourself, you may wish to sign yourself into a hospital as a way of protecting yourself against these impulses. If you decide to go through with the suicide, please call me first and cancel your next appointment so that I can use the time some other way." Ram Dass suggests:

> Compassion without pity . . . somebody calls up and says, "This is horrible and I'm going to commit suicide." I say, "Well, then

don't let me keep you. If you've got to go do that, you do whatever
you need to do. But I just want you to know I'm here if you want
to hang out for a while before you commit suicide. Since you're
going to do it anyway, you know what you've got to do, but if
you'd like to hang out, here we are."[7]

I once made a lavish effort to save a patient from suicide.
Unwittingly playing the part of his unsuccessful rescuer, I arranged
joint therapy sessions with the patient and his wife, and his parents,
and his employer. All of our combined efforts failed to stop him
from killing himself. In retrospect, I believe that all we accomplished was to make the entire transaction more melodramatic.
In twenty-five years of practice, he has been my only successful
suicidal patient, so far.

The therapeutic impasse can arise as easily out of negative
attachment to the pain of hostility, as out of the positive attachment
to the pleasure of sex. Feeling that I cannot possibly bear a painful
experience is as binding as insistence that I simply cannot do
without a pleasurable one. Concentration on the Work allows the
therapist liberation from both kinds of impasses.

Chapter 8

Phases and Basic Interventions

Each phase of the practice of Yoga marks an attained stage in development of the Yogi's own spiritual condition. Because of this identity of program and process, Yoga is *not* quite right as a metaphor for the patient's development in the course of psychotherapy.

The patient comes to psychotherapy hoping to attain greater happiness by resolving troubling emotional problems. The Therapeutic Process of increasing self awareness is chosen as a path he or she hopes will lead to this goal. Like the Yogi, the patient may go on to complete the three phases of this process. But unlike the Yogi, though the development of what the patient is seeking may be facilitated by participation in the formal process, it will *not* be identical with that process. The patient's progress in resolving emotional conflicts will *not* reflect a step-by-step parallel with the unfolding of the Therapeutic Process.

During the movement through the Opening Phase (I), the Middle Phase (II), and the Termination Phase (III) of psychotherapy, the patient may not *complete* the work of attaining the improved psychological condition that he or she seeks. On the other hand, this goal may be attained *before* finishing the last phase of psychotherapy. The patient may then go on to complete the Therapeutic Process for other reasons.

Recognition that the patient's personal quest for happiness is *separate* from the Work of the Therapeutic Process is crucial for the therapist. It allows the therapist to give oneself over to concentration on the technical aspects of the Work unhampered by any attachment to the patient's goal of making progress in resolving emotional problems.

As the therapist I am *not* there to help solve the patient's problems. My task is the mediating of the Therapeutic Process by promoting the patient's growing awareness. I work toward facilitating the patient's self-understanding. If I do my job well, the patient becomes clearer about his or her own acts, thoughts, feelings, and wishes.

The patient learns more about the process, the rewards, and the costs of a particular way of living. What he or she chooses to do with this increased consciousness is up to the patient. It need not be of any particular interest to me. I am in charge of conducting the Therapeutic Process, leaving the patient completely in charge of running his or her own life.

There are two major aspects to the therapist's work in promoting the Therapeutic Process. The first lies in the creation of an atmosphere of safety and freedom for the patient. This nurturant atmosphere is produced by the understanding and respect communicated by the therapist's posture of non-judgmental, acceptingly attentive listening. Unattached to the *outcome* of the process for the patient, the therapist is free *not* to meddle. I mind my own business by concentrating on doing the work I am paid to do.

The patient in turn is free to talk about anything he or she wishes. With this comes the freedom to keep private anything the patient chooses not to disclose. The therapist speaks *only* when there is something to say that is believed will be useful in promoting the ongoing Therapeutic Process.

To the extent that the therapist has successfully created an accepting atmosphere, the patient can be trusted to choose and to explore what is meaningful at any given point. The therapist need only intervene when the patient's participation in the Therapeutic Process has been interrupted.

Interruptions in the stream of the patient's expanding consciousness occur when it comes to the threshold of some piece of awareness that is too disturbing, too confounding, or too painful to permit going on. Whether consciously or unconsciously, the patient's heightened anxiety calls forth characteristic defenses that stem the movement of the Therapeutic Process.

Any interruption in the Process can be extremely frustrating to a therapist who judges the Work in terms of how the patient is progressing. The therapist's attachment to results can transform the patient's internal struggle into a power-locked impasse *between* them.

It is little wonder that traditionally therapists have referred to such interruptions in the patient's flow of associations as "*Resist-*

ance." The term denotes unconstructive, self-protective defensiveness on the part of the patient as (conscious or unconscious) fighting against being "cured" by the psychotherapist. These defensive attitudes and behaviors have been thought of as arising when the impact of therapeutic intervention heightens the patient's awareness of previously-repressed material. So great is the patient's anxiety about underlying conflicts that it becomes more than he or she can bear. With personality, value system, and particularly with neurosis under attack, the patient was thought to rebel against, or at least to retreat from these threats. This was understood to be carried on by deliberately or unwittingly throwing up smoke screens and camouflages to confuse the therapist and to block progress. Despite the allegedly unconscious nature of some of the "resistances," their designation implies the traditional therapist's blaming the patient for not getting on with it.

Among those attitudes and behaviors usually included in the category of "resistance" are the full gamut of phenomena that call forth feelings of helplessness in the psychotherapist who is trying to *make* the patient change. Such "resistances" include suppression and repression, intensification of symptoms, self-devaluation, flight into health, intellectualization, acting-out, superficial talk, "contempt for normality" (!), lateness, absences, nonpayment of bills, etc.[1]

Where the traditional concept of "resistance" is primary in the thinking of the therapist, it is the patient who is seen as responsible for anything that goes wrong. It makes more sense to me to reserve the term "resistance" for those sane, creative, realistically self-protective attitudes and behaviors the patient uses to cope with the errors perpetrated by the therapist. These "resistances" are signals to the therapist that the patient is not getting what is needed to move along in the Therapeutic Process.

Not that every pause needs to be seen as a defensive stoppage. There is a tidal rhythm to the Therapeutic Process. After any surge of new awareness and the emotional crisis that attends such transformations, the patient may need a period of rest and calm. Quiet interludes of this sort allow restoration of psychic balance, integration of new material, and regathering of inner powers to move on.

When it appears that it is the patient's anxiety that is causing the halting or straying from concentration on the Therapeutic Process, the therapist has the opportunity to offer a meaningful intervention. If the intervention is correct, and the timing is right, the therapist's work serves to restore and promote resumption of the patient's full participation in that process. In its own way, each intervention is an encroachment on the activity and the freedom of the patient. The therapist's goal of impeccable work demands that therapeutic interventions be offered *only* when they are needed to facilitate the patient's freedom to go on with his or her own quest.

Whether or not an intervention is the correct one, offered at the right time, cannot be judged simply in terms of the patient's direct conscious agreement or disagreement. The therapist must judge the correctness or error of any particular intervention only in terms of the renewal of the flow of the Therapeutic Process.[2]

Just because a patient disagrees directly with an intervention by the therapist does *not* necessarily mean that it was incorrect. Conversely, the patient's immediate agreement with an intervention should not be taken as definitely confirming the correctness of the work.

The crucial factor in confirmation of an intervention is the material that follows the patient's initial comments. A therapist need not consider an interpretation or any other intervention to be valid *unless* the patient's subsequent behavior lends it confirmation.

If the intervention is correct it will serve to free up the patient from the stuck place in which he or she is embedded. At that point the Therapeutic Process moves on freely once more. Direct confirmation from the patient comes in the form of new and fresh material of many kinds. These will include the recall of previously repressed material such as dreams, fantasies, and childhood memories. The fresh material will *not* appear completely out of context. It is likely to be related to earlier more superficial and general contents on which considerable previous therapeutic work has already been done.

When the intervention is confirmed as being on the mark, the patient's growing awareness will usually provide new, related materials and fresh leads to other aspects of the problem. These may include other experiences and fantasies that the patient had not yet talked about in the therapy. New awareness also provides opportunities for the integration of matters already discussed but not yet understood.

When fresh material does arise to confirm an intervention, it will usually be the focus of subsequent work in the sessions that follow. These deeper understandings can only take place at a time when the patient is *ready* to become aware of, to reveal, and to explore related feelings, ideas, and memories. The newly-remembered confirming material will fit with earlier material and will have a quality of spontaneity. It is likely to contribute to further understanding of previously-unexplored aspects of the patient's personality.

Confirmation of an intervention may be indirect or delayed. If indirect, the patient's response may be expressed in a derivative reference to some earlier time in treatment when something the therapist said turned out to be useful. Or a step removed from that, the patient may suddenly remember and talk about someone else who *really* listens and understands.

All of this may occur later in that session or in subsequent sessions. Derivative distance from the original material and delays in expressing confirmation usually suggests that the intervention, while correct, pointed to a very complex and sensitive area with which the patient was not yet ready to deal fully and directly.

Should the patient disagree with an interpretation or some other type of intervention, the therapist must *never* attempt to persuade, to argue, or to justify the intervention. Instead the therapist must accept the negative response, silently reconsider the formulation, and listen!

After a while the validity of the intervention can be assessed in terms of what the patient has to say. Even after the patient's disagreement, the delayed emergence of new and fresh material can be taken as a confirmation of the intervention.

Whether the patient agrees or disagrees, non-confirming material may emerge. In that case even if the patient has agreed to the interpretation, the intervention was incorrect.

The quality of non-confirming responses is that they are stale and empty, lacking in vitality. Nothing comes together. No new or freshly-viewed material emerges. The patient remains silent and lost, or ruminates in a shallow and trivial way. The patient does *not* talk about feelings, but about thoughts *about* feelings. Attention is concentrated on superficial circumstantial problems and events.

The therapist's error may be based on a countertransference problem. It may arise out of a technical misunderstanding of the patient and of the work required at that point. In either case, the therapist must continue to listen to the patient.

Every therapist spends most of each session having to tolerate not understanding what's going on. The Work in each session is a series of errors and corrections, as the therapist offers approximations that gradually move closer and closer to deep empathy with the patient.

Defending or elaborating on unconfirmed interventions leads to a therapist-dominated misalliance. "Persuading" the patient creates a critical, unaccepting, and unsafe atmosphere in which the Therapeutic Process cannot be sustained. If the therapist listens carefully, the patient will often unconsciously redirect attention toward the correct intervention.

Consider this admittedly oversimplified example. For several sessions a female patient has been discussing with a male therapist how poorly she and her parents get along. She has just learned that they are planning to fly to Europe for an extended vacation.

P: "I know that today flying is safer than traveling by automobile. Still I can't shake the panicky feeling that my folks might get killed in an airplane crash over the ocean. I haven't said anything to them about it but I've been worried sick since they told me they were going to Europe."

T: "You've been talking about how badly you and your folks get along. You've felt so angry at them that perhaps you secretly wish that their plane *would* crash. Then you wouldn't have to bother with them any more."

P: "I'm sure I'm not *that* angry at them." (*Disagrees directly.*)

T: "It's hard for you to accept that you could be angry enough to want them dead. But you know that fears are sometimes nothing but wishes turned inside out." (*Pushes and justifies the interpretation.*)

P: "Well, I guess unconsciously I might have that wish. I know

that the Unconscious can play funny tricks on a person's mind
. . ." (*Patient appeases the therapist and goes on with non-confirm-*
ing obsessing about the matter.) You know it feels so lonely to
have an Unconscious so removed from my everyday self. Sometimes
I'm so out of touch with my self I don't know what I'm really
trying to say."

The reader who is carefully attending to the patient's last
statement may begin to become aware that the issue is not anger,
but abandonment. Unconsciously the patient is telling the therapist
about her two major related concerns of the moment.

The first is that she and her parents do not get along because
they do not listen to her enough to understand what she is feeling.
Her fear about the plane crash is *not* a death wish, but her dread
of losing them totally.

She is also letting the therapist know about her loneliness with
him. He, too, has not listened. He, too, does not understand.
Unconsciously she is trying to cure him of this. If he attends
to what she is saying without defending himself against the message,
she will redirect him onto the right track.

It is crucial to remember that a patient is in a sound position
to make a valid negation of any intervention. Some therapists believe
that if a patient contests an intervention, this is being defensive.
Such a therapist denies the respect merited by the patient as a
source of valid criticism of the therapist's work. The patient's
non-confirmation or objection to the intervention is considered
to be nothing more than neurotic resistance.

Non-confirming responses by the patient to any given intervention can take many forms. Acute symptoms (often psychosomatic)
may arise during or after the session. The patient may get involved
in dramatic acting out, either within the session or right after
it. (By "acting out," I mean short-sightedly adaptive behavior that
momentarily solves a conflict, avoids awareness of feelings, and
often creates new problems. Examples might include dealing with
feeling upset by running away, staging a fight, giving a gift, etc.)

In the process of acting out, the patient may become confused,
intimidated, and show the poor judgment that goes with feeling
overwhelmed. Disturbance of the therapeutic alliance may result
in the patient's becoming seductive, or attacking the therapist.

If the impasse continues, the patient may begin to withdraw by coming late, missing sessions, and by threatening to terminate, or by actually terminating prematurely.

Whether conscious or unconscious, the patient's response to the fact that the therapist has *not* understood, or has missed something will usually persist. Derivatives of material that the therapist has failed to meet with the called-for intervention will continue to appear.

The Work pivots around understanding communications from the patient and facilitating growing understanding of the self. This process must be viewed partly in terms of the patient's struggle to deal with the impact of input from interventions offered by the therapist as well as from the Unconscious and from intervening life experiences. Robert Langs' model for these interactions within the microcosm of each psychotherapy session provides a very helpful overview:

> Simply and ideally, a psychotherapy session has the following basic structure. Its foundation lies in the previous session and the reality experiences that have occurred since then. The session itself begins with the patient talking about whatever is on his mind, thereby developing the major theme of the hour, and defining his current primary adaptive tasks and his reactions to them on all levels. These initial communications are both verbal and non-verbal. The therapist listens to the manifest and latent content, formulates, and checks out these assessments as the patient goes on, revising his hypotheses accordingly. At an appropriate moment in the session, the therapist makes an intervention. The patient responds verbally and non-verbally, and associates further, either confirming the intervention or failing to do so.[3]

Though the sessions do have a definite point of beginning and of ending, they are arbitrary slices of the patient's ongoing life. The therapist may be tempted to read into them a structure that is more conceptual than real. The categorizing of the Therapeutic Process into Phases I, II, and III; the defining of the stages within any given session can be useful only if we are not misled into making them into realities.

All of this categorization is merely a conceptual device developed to provide a practical way of thinking about an otherwise too fluid rush of experience. It is "a fictional hedge to be raised at those times when we feel that we can no longer stand working in the boundlessly flowing stream of the ever-changing process of live interactions with another separate human being. It offers the therapist the momentarily soothing illusion of order in the overwhelming chaos of ongoing life."[4] These categorizations are as arbitrary as any conceptual orderings of the life process. They are as gratuitous, though not nearly so useful, as defining a person's development as though there were real and clear-cut stages of infancy, childhood, adolescence, young adulthood, middle age, and old age.

We therapists speak to each other with conviction about a patient being immersed in predictable Phase II transference reactions. Another patient is described as clearly caught up in a typical Phase I impasse. Yet another patient is described as doing characteristic Phase III work.

Privately, we know that often we cannot tell just which phase a patient is in. Even when a particular phase seems to have been entered, worked through, and left behind, we find that some of the same configurations emerge again and again in the next phase.

In theory it all seems so clear. In practice, all too often, the differences between one phase and the next are *not* at all clear.

In describing these Phases of the Therapeutic Process, I discuss the themes, impasses, and interventions that occur in each particular stage. These distinctions are useful as guidelines *only* when I remember that they represent no more than a simplified map of a complex territory.

Some themes seem to dominate one phase more than they do another. A particular impasse appears to characterize each phase. Certain therapeutic interventions are more often called for at one stage of treatment than they are in the other two.

But as all working therapists know, *each* motif, struggle, and technical resolution occurs in *every* phase. Even so, many of us find it helpful to recognize that any one of these parameters may be found more typically in the foreground of one phase of therapy than in the others.

In discussing the basic therapeutic interventions that predominate in each of the three phases of treatment, I have *not* covered any of the valuable specialized techniques. Approaches such as bio-energetics,[5] guided fantasy,[6] gestalt dream-work,[7] and the like have been well-developed elsewhere in the therapeutic literature.

I would like to point out that when I *do* introduce any of these exotic techniques into my own work, I do so in the context of the analysis of changes in therapeutic parameters. A therapeutic bag of tricks is no substitute for a sound alliance between patient and therapist. I offer these techniques within an atmosphere of trust, and never push them on the patient. I introduce them as opportunities for willing participation and I set them aside if the patient does not feel safe enough to try them.

These innovative interventions can promote dramatic break-throughs of insight and feelings. These will be of no lasting value if the patient is not ready for the new awareness. Later the patient will need to be helped to take these changes and work them through into becoming a part of his or her everyday experience.

The momentary awakenings provided by such techniques are not to be confused with the hard-won, long-term personal gains of disciplined and repeated re-examination provided by the Therapeutic Process. The distinction is parallel to that of the sudden satori of the acid trip compared with the spiritual liberation that only comes with years of daily Yoga meditation.

PHASE I

During the opening phase of therapy, the therapist and the patient do not yet know each other well enough for the Therapeutic Process to be mediated by the intimacy of relationship that they may some day achieve. Nor has the patient begun to be sufficiently self-aware to be able to depend on the guidance of the Unconscious.

More than any other stage of treatment, Phase I depends on disciplined technical work by the therapist. Because of this empha-sis, it is the easiest phase to teach and to write about, though not necessarily the easiest one to learn to conduct.

This first phase lasts from a few weeks to a few months. During this period the presenting symptoms usually disappear as the patient shifts attention by becoming curious about the rest of his or her life. This comes about through a shift in attention away from complaints and onto the Therapeutic Process.

The three primary areas of concentration in Phase I are: the establishing of the therapeutic alliance, the analysis of the patient's style, and the redefining of the problems. Each theme calls for the predominating use of a particular set of therapeutic interventions.

In the relationship, the central issue is *trust*. The required intervention is the *reflection of feelings*.

An understanding of *neurotic style* requires character analytic work. For this exploration, *confrontation* is the main type of intervention.

The patient starts out with a self-image of a neurotic with symptoms or as a victim of unkind Fate. The third theme is the *redefining of these problems*. It involves a transformation of the patient's self-image into that of an ordinary human being who would like to live a happier life. The mediating intervention by the therapist is that of *structural questioning*.

The foundation of the therapeutic alliance is that of *trust*. How is the therapist to communicate to the patient that he or she is an attentive, understanding listener who is ready to respect the patient's feelings and beliefs?

Trust cannot be established simply by telling the patient: "I hear you. I understand. I care." What the therapist does, not what he or she *says*, becomes the basis for the patient's experiencing the safe, nurturant atmosphere within which the Therapeutic Process can thrive. It depends totally on how the patient is treated.

If the patient is to be able to establish a trusting working alliance with the therapist, there must be an *experience* of really being listened to and understood. Ironically, the therapist attempting to establish this trust during Phase I is only beginning to know the patient. I need to communicate some sense of understanding just at that time when I understand the patient least.

Busy formulating hypotheses in my head about the nature of the patient's problems, I may be tempted to show I understand by offering interpretations of the underlying meaning of the patient's behavior. This is a mistake. Even if some of my interpretations are correct, they are likely to be premature. If a patient is not ready to receive the awareness that might later come with a well-timed interpretation, the impact is more likely to be one of feeling assaulted than understood. Deep interpretations are to be avoided during Phase I.

The kind of understanding that encourages trust during this phase is attained by the therapist's depending heavily on the therapeutic intervention called *Reflection of Feelings.* I listen carefully to what is being described about the patient's life situation, sense of self, or experience of being in therapy. Attempting to put myself in the patient's place, I then formulate what seems to be the central *feeling* that the patient is expressing. It is this feeling that I reflect back to the patient in a way that heightens awareness of what is being experienced.

This intervention of reflecting feelings was developed by Carl Rogers many years ago as the central technique of his then revolutionary Client-Centered Psychotherapy.[8]

> Early in his work, Rogers grew dissatisfied with having the counselor's role defined as distant and superior, as the expert authority who handed down interpretations. He saw the client and the therapist as equals, and so felt that the therapist's attitude should be respectful, open, and permissive. The therapist's orientation must be phenomenological in that concern must be for the world as the client experiences it, rather than for "reality" (compared with what?) or as a screen for the "hidden" unconscious dynamics. In fact, Rogers felt that any diagnostic assumptions about the client would be presumptuous and detrimental. Instead the non-directive therapist treats the patient with "unconditional positive regard" and respects the client's feelings. He can show the client he is understood, and help him to understand his own feelings more clearly by reflecting back in a non-judgmental way, what the client has said. In such an atmosphere, Rogers believes the client will solve his own problems.[9]

The term "reflection" turned out to be an unfortunate label for this intervention. Young therapists have sometimes taken it to mean that what is required is a simple *mirroring* of what the patient is saying. An apocryphal "dialogue" makes this point painfully clear:

P: "Doctor I'm having lots of trouble."

T: "You feel that you are having lots of trouble."

P: "My life is rotten. I'm a miserable failure."

T: "You feel that your life is rotten and that you're a miserable failure."

P: "It just doesn't seem like there's anything worth living for."

T: "You feel that there's nothing worth living for."

P: (*Patient gets up out of his chair, goes to the open window of the therapist's office. He jumps out of the window, screaming as he falls.*) "Ahhhh. . . ."

T: "Ahhhh. . . ."

The problem here is twofold. The therapist in this vignette does nothing more than echo the patient's words. He is without appreciation of what it must be like to be in the patient's situation. No empathy is communicated. There is evidence of careful listening to the patient's words, but failure to show any understanding of the patient's experience. As the therapist, I must try to appreciate what it might be like to be in the patient's place. I need *not* feel *sympathy* with the patient's attitude in order to be able to identify with it.

The therapist must try to appreciate not only the patient's words, but who it is who speaks these words. I try to sense what it feels like to be the patient and what it must feel like to be telling all this to a stranger. What I need to be able to communicate my empathy is a certain freshness to the feedback. I must be able to summarize in new words the central feeling behind the patient's statements. Only this will show that the patient has really been heard. This freshness may even deepen the patient's own understanding of what is being felt.

There is a wonderful example of the work of the reflection of feelings at its best on Carl Rogers' famous tape, "Mr. Vac."[10] It would be necessary for the reader to listen to the tape or to watch Rogers at work in order to appreciate fully the depth of caring and commitment communicated to the patient by Rogers' tone of voice.

The interviews with Mr. Vac were a part of a project offering individual psychotherapy to hospitalized schizophrenics. These patients are described as:

> . . . individuals who do not know what psychotherapy is, who probably would not choose it if they did know, who are often of low socio-educational status, who feel no conscious need for help.[11]

The psychotherapy sessions with these patients consisted mostly of *silence!* Mr. Vac is a man in his late 20s with two previous hospitalizations. At the time of this interview he had been recommitted for over two years, diagnosed as Schizophrenic Reaction, Simple Type. When the session from which I will quote took place, Mr. Vac had been seen twice a week for a period of eleven months. Late in that session which up to now has included over 30 minutes of intermittent silence, the following series of exchanges take place:

P: I just ain't no good to nobody, never was, and never will be.

T: Feeling that now, huh? That you're just no good to yourself, no good to anybody. Never will be any good to anybody. Just that you're completely worthless, huh? . . . Those really are lousy feelings. Just feel that you're no good at *all*, huh?

P: Yeah. That's what this guy I went to town with just the other day told me.

T: This guy that you went to town with really told you that you were no good? Is that what you're saying? Did I get that right?

P: Uh, hum.

T: I guess the meaning of that if I get it right is that here's somebody that . . . meant something to you and what does he think of you? Why, he's told you that he thinks you're no good at all. And that just really knocks the props out from you.

P: (weeps quietly)

T: It just brings the tears. (Silence of 20 seconds)

P: I don't care though.

T: You tell yourself you don't care at all, but somehow I guess some part of you cares because some part of you weeps over it. (Silence of 19 seconds)

T: I guess some part of you just feels, "Here I am hit with another blow, as if I hadn't had enough blows like this during my life when I feel that people don't like me. Here's someone I've begun to feel attached to and now *he* doesn't like me. And I'll say I don't care. I won't let it make any difference to me . . . But just the same the tears run down my cheeks."

P: I guess I always knew it.

T: Hm?

P: I guess I always knew it.

T: If I'm getting that right, it is that what makes it hurt worst of all is that when he tells you you're no good, well shucks, that's what you've always felt about yourself. Is that . . . the meaning of what you're saying? . . . Uh, hum, So you feel as though he's just confirming what you've already felt in some way. (Silence of 23 seconds)

T: So that between his saying so and your perhaps feeling it underneath, you just feel about as no good as anybody could feel. (Silence of 2 minutes, 1 second)

T: And I sorta let it soak in and try to feel what you must be feeling . . . it comes up sorta this way in me and I don't know,—but as though here was someone you'd made a contact with, someone you'd really done things for and done things with. Somebody that had some meaning to you. Now, wow! He slaps you in the face by telling you you're just no good. And this really cuts *so* deep, you can hardly stand it.[12]

During Phase I, reflection of feelings is the called-for intervention whenever the patient has completed reporting some segment of description of a life situation, an inner state, or of the relationship with the therapist. This will result in a deepening of the patient's experience of his own feelings, a continuing flow of fresh material, and a gradual building of trust in the therapeutic alliance.

However, it will soon become evident to the therapist that sometimes the reflections are absorbed without apparent impact. The very *manner* in which the patient attempts to respond to the intervention, itself prevents broader or deeper exploration of what is going on inside.

The patient may go on to introduce additional content but all of it will be presented in a characteristic *style* that by its very nature serves to limit any further self-awareness. This impasse constitutes the emergence of *neurotic character style.* The called-for intervention is *confrontation.* The work at this point requires that the therapist shift concentration from content to form, by focusing away from *what* is being said, to *how* it is being said.

In his seminal work on character analysis, Wilhelm Reich points out that:

> . . . the patient must first find out *that* he defends himself, then by what means, . . . [and] finally, against what.[13]

It works best to hold off on this confrontational character analysis for the first few sessions to give the patient's full style a chance to surface. The patient will be consciously putting forward symptoms and life problems in hope of discussing, exploring, and resolving them.

In contrast, the character style will simply be lived out, often without awareness. Even if partially conscious of this manner, the patient is unlikely to understand all of the ways in which it restricts the range of his or her experience. Should there be awareness of some aspects of this style and dissatisfaction with some of its effects, it is still unlikely to be viewed as a problem about which anything can be done. No matter how aware or dissatisfied a person is with this character style, it is likely to be experienced as a fact of nature. For the patient, it is just the way he or she is.

The patient's stylized approach may be an unwittingly self-limiting attitude of skepticism, intellectualization, and detachment. It may instead be one of compliance, passivity, and disinterest, or of denial, shallowness, and unfounded optimism. The variety of character configurations are many.

Whatever the variations, all neurotic character styles have certain common characteristics.[14] Such styles are protective attitudes developed early in life as necessary armor against an emotionally destructive environment. At first they served to keep the patient safe from the surrounding dangers. Additionally they offer protection against internal anguish too overwhelming to be borne at the time.

Now in adult life these attitudes are self-maintaining. In limiting the patient's experience of anxiety, they restrict the possibilities for new experience. Ironically, in this way they prevent realization that the original danger is past.

As with all avoidant defenses, these have been set up to hold off catastrophe. Unexpected experiences and risky behaviors are limited. The patient does not do anything new and "dangerous." The prohibited act is avoided. The unconsciously dreaded terrible consequences do *not* come about. Thus every bit of avoidant behavior is reinforced by the absence of consequent catastrophe.

Dealing with the patient's neurotic style is a twofold problem for the therapist. If the necessary confrontational work of character analysis is *not* done first, all of the subsequent interpretative interventions of Phase II will do nothing to promote the Therapeutic Process. For example, I may make the error of neglecting this Phase I work with an obsessional patient. I go on with her into what I mistakenly take to be Phase II of our misalliance. Not having recognized and worked through her neurotic style, she continues intellectualizing all of her experiences in a way that protects her from fear of losing control of her feelings. The result is that my Phase II interpretations simply facilitate her becoming the most insightful neurotic in the Washington metropolitan area.

A second oversimplified example could involve my negligence in this Phase I work with an hysteric. Neglecting to confront him about his style of romantic denial of bad feelings, I participate in the mutually-seductive misalliance of our both being very special creatures. The Phase II interpretations result in seemingly miraculous transformations of the patient. These changes turn out to be as unstable as our ability to maintain the magic of our union.

A second aspect of the problem for the therapist doing this work is the fact that character analysis cannot be forced. Necessary as it is to the promotion of the Therapeutic Process, confrontation cannot be carried out as a form of coercion. Confrontation is *not* challenge, and must *never* be punitive. This unfortunately labelled intervention is no more than the therapist's inviting attention to a previously-ignored pattern of the patient's behavior so that awareness of it may be increased. It is true that observed behavior is always somewhat different than unobserved behavior. Still, any basic change in style can result only from the patient's curiosity about it; curiosity based on growing understanding of this style, of its origins, and of the costs of this protection.

At worst, confrontation can be misused by the therapist to criticize how the patient behaves and to try to force change. In its most extreme form, this constitutes the basic intervention of the attack therapy of the Synanon-style of self-help for drug addicts, the aggression therapy of George Bach, and the barnstorming workshops of certain itinerant encounter group leaders.

A clear example of this misuse of confrontation is described as a Synanon method for "attacking the [phony] insight discovery."

"Well, in the Synanon, we confronted Lefty with his atrocious behavior. He began to use a psychological mishmash of terms to defend. He said that he had a psychological block, that he was displacing aggression, and a whole bunch of other rationalizations and bullshit.

"Chuck and I glanced at each other and decided to really put him on. Chuck said something like, "Well, let's examine the psychological implication of your behavior with Bill.' Lefty brightened up, and we went at it. Chuck said, 'Let's analyze it. Is there any significant figure in your earlier life or is there any situation that comes to you mind when you think about the Crawford incident?'

"Lefty's eyes began to glitter, and he said, 'Let me think.' Chuck saw him take the bait and said, 'This may explain the whole thing, think hard.' Lefty pursed his lips, acted pained, wrinkled his brow, stared up at the ceiling, and went off into a reverie of deep thought.

"He then said, 'Gee, that makes a lot of sense. It certainly brings something to my consciousness. At one period, when I was a kid, and I use to wash dishes—'

"'Who did you wash dishes for?'

"'It was my grandmother! She had a certain way of talking to me and a nasal twang and . . .'

"'And perhaps this reminds you of Crawford?'

"'That's it! Crawford sounds just like my grandmother. She use to make me wash dishes and nag at me when I wanted to go out and play. She really used to incite my hostility.'

"Then Chuck said, 'Well maybe we've hit on it. Crawford, with his particular approach and his voice tone, seems to trigger you, and you associate his behavior with hers.' Everyone in the session joined in to confirm Lefty's exciting insight discovery.

"Lefty picked up on the group's approval and went on further: 'By God, that's it exactly—when Crawford comes on like he does, it's my grandmother all over again. No wonder I blow up and . . .'

"At this point Lefty was beaming—carrying on and everything— and then Chuck pushed him right off the cliff. 'You lying son-of-a-bitch, you're so full of shit, it's ridiculous!' With that, everyone in the group broke up in a loud roar of laughter.[15]

Confrontations need never be punitive, blaming, or còercive. The therapeutic intervention of confrontation involves my calling the patient's attention to observable aspects of behavior that have been ignored up to that point. This is done simply by way of my offering my observations without blame or criticism. It is a way of directing the patient's attention to *how* he or she behaves. The purpose is to promote the Therapeutic Process by increasing self-awareness. I make no effort to judge the behavior, nor to suggest that it be changed in any way.

These observations are most effectively offered by juxtaposing a number of pieces of behavior that go together to reflect the patient's characteristic attitudinal style. My primary focus is on how the patient behaves within the therapy sessions. Examples must be concrete and directly observable. Later I can go on to point out how the patient's style is reflected in daily life by pointing out similar behavior in reports of interactions with other people.

In order to convey some sense of the accepting and respectful confrontational interventions required for Phase I character analytic work, I will present a condensed, somewhat idealized set of transactions between a male patient and his therapist. The reader will need to understand that this interplay condenses work carried out over the course of many weeks. The actual process is fraught with therapist errors, false starts, unexpected impasses, and intervening materials from the patient that are not directly related to the character analysis.

P: I had a lot of trouble at work last week. The boss told me to inventory the stock. Then some emergency deliveries had to be made so I went out to do them. When I got back I was ready to get on with completing the inventory. It had to be done in a hurry. I was way behind schedule by then. But no sooner had I gotten started, than the assistant boss got back from out of town. I had to take time out to help him catch up on things. By Friday I still hadn't finished the inventory. The boss was mad at me because of that. And the assistant boss told me I was so tense that I wasn't much help in getting him caught up either.

T: You had an awful lot of work to do this week. You tried your best but it was just too much to do. And then you ended up feeling even worse because your bosses were both dissatisfied with you. (*Attempts to reflect patient's feelings.*)

P: Well, they were right. I messed everything up because I just didn't work fast enough. I've never been able to please the people I've worked for. (*Rejects reflection in favor of self-critical explanation.*)

T: Underneath your complaining about yourself, you must be very angry at the bosses for demanding that you do more than anyone could manage. (*Unwarranted premature interpretation.*)

P: Why should I get angry at them? I just feel guilty because I haven't done my job. (*Rejects interpretation. Returns to self-blaming.*)

T: I've noticed that no matter what you're telling me about, you always talk in an apologetic voice. Your sholders sag and your head is lowered. You shake your head as if your are exasperated with yourself, and sometimes you roll your eyes as though you can't believe what a fuck-up you think you are. (*Confrontation.*)

P: I guess I do. I hadn't thought of it that way before. You're right to criticize me for that. It's a dumb way to look and to sound. It must make a lousy impression. I should know better.

T: You hear my observations as criticism. You're telling me right now that you are to blame for being so hard on yourself, even though you weren't aware that that's how you present yourself when you talk to me.

P: I guess I feel ashamed to tell you about how many ways I screw things up.

T: You've told me several stories about times when you and your bosses weren't getting along at work, and when you and your parents weren't getting along at home. (*Cites concrete examples.*) In every story, no matter what has gone wrong, you always tell it apologetically as though it's your fault, as though you are the guilty party. (*Expands scope of confrontation.*)

P: I guess I do that a lot. Without realizing it, I guess I'm always acting like I know it's all my fault. I wonder why I act that way.

T: You begin to see that putting yourself down is the way

that you approach most conflicts. You're becoming aware that there must be something behind the way that your manner pleads you guilty, even before you are accused of being to blame. You don't know the underlying reason yet, but you can see that it has an effect on all of our talks. Even my observations about your behavior seem like criticisms to you that confirm just how bad you feel about yourself.

This confrontational structuring of patient's beginning awareness of his character style would actually be built up over many sessions, a bit at a time. In that way the didactic tone of the therapist's last response would be avoided.

At this point the correct timing of the confrontation would be confirmed if the patient retold one of the stories in a fresh way that did not assume his own guilt in advance. If the character armoring was not too heavy, some of his underlying feelings might begin to emerge. Another likely possibility would be that new memories might come to mind. These would reveal early experiences and relationships in which this character formation originally took root.

In practice, confrontations such as this one must be made again and again throughout Phase I (and later if needed). The *content* of *what* is being told must be ignored in favor of concentrating on the *form* of *how* it is being told.

With a patient like this man, if the character work is not substantially accomplished during the first phase of the treatment, the result will be a sado-masochistic misalliance. The Therapeutic Process then deteriorates into a stale, predictable sequence of confessions by the patient, with the therapist underscoring his faults and the patient making new penitential resolutions to change. By then I would have found myself in the position of judging, condemning therapist/parent of this unsatisfactory fuck-up of a patient/son.

This young man's penitential, self-blaming character style pervades his behavior and colors everything he experiences. Yet it is the only aspect of himself with which he is not dissatisfied. He must become aware that he has such a style before he can learn that it influences how he understands his life and what he communicates of himself to others.

Only then can he deepen his immersion in the Therapeutic Process by becoming conscious that his life-style is that of an accused man pleading guilty to a lesser charge in order to avoid being punished for a more serious offense. His plea-bargaining involves continual confession to the misdemeanor of conscious Inadequacy in order to beat the felony counts of unconscious Rage and Pride. By copping a plea to being a fuck-up, he hides from himself and from others both his murderous rage against those in authority, and his grandiose superiority toward everyone else. His perfectionist standards require that he be able to do whatever is demanded of him. Lower standards obtain for lesser beings.

The character analytic work required with any particular patient cannot be carried out effectively outside the context of the growing trust required for a sound therapeutic alliance. Trust in this alliance allows the character work to open the patient to new ways of experiencing. At that point I can introduce the third focus of Phase I work: the redefining of the patient's problems. This work requires the intervention of *structural questioning*.

A therapist may ask a patient many questions in order to clarify a communication, or merely to get more information. It may not be clear that all of these questions direct the patient to regard some facts or feelings as more important than others. Seemingly simple questions lead the patient in irrelevant directions which might not otherwise be pursued. Consider the therapist's superficially innocuous attempts to obtain additional historical data such as: "How old were you at the time?" or "Were all of the children in the family treated that way?"

Because of the unintended implicit burden that the therapist's questions may place on the patient, some therapists try to avoid questions completely. An apocryphal tale is told of a group therapist who was participating in a weekend encounter group workshop. He was enormously impressed with the forceful leadership of the man who was running the encounter group. As the weekend went on he realized that the leader's power seemed to lie in the fact that he *never* asked any questions of the group members.

Returning to his practice the following week, the group therapist decided to try to increase his own therapeutic effectiveness by emulating the encounter group leader's question-free approach. The first time that the therapy group he led met that week, he felt very excited. He began the session by describing to them his experience of the weekend, his recognition of the powerful non-questioning technique of the encounter group leader, and his intention to work in the same way. He concluded this statement to the group by saying: "From now on I am never, never again going to ask any questions of you people. How does that strike you?"

The majority of therapists find that:

> In most therapy sessions . . ., it is not possible to go very long without having to ask a question.[16]

The point then is to recognize the question as a valid therapeutic intervention. As such, it is to be used deliberately, only when called for, and with the express purpose of promoting the patient's participation in the Therapeutic Process. As such, the goal is increasing the patient's understanding, *not* the therapist's.

Structural questioning in particular is the called-for intervention late in Phase I, at a time when the patient is describing life problems in neurotic terms. The patient defines the self as the problem (e.g., "I am inadequate, unworthy, unlovable, etc."). Nonexistent solutions to these created problems become the futile focus. Neurosis is not a matter of personal defects. It is largely a problem of attention.

Focused on a sense that there is something wrong with him or her, the patient has lost sight of the richness of possibilities in the ongoing process of life. The purpose of the intervention of structural questioning is to shift attention to the fullness and complexity of a life seen only in terms of the impoverished verbal model inside the patient's head. Because of narrowed attention, conscious representation of life suffers from missing parts, unexamined presuppositions, and costly distortions.[17,18]

The following examples of structural questioning will be presented in a single sequence, with each question occurring only once. In practice, these interventions are repeated along the way over more than one session. Each time a particular question is asked it redirects the patient's attention away from the surface structure of complaints about self-image toward expansion of awareness of some aspect of the underlying deep structure.

The patient in this instance is a high school senior still living at home with his parents and three younger brothers.

P: My trouble is that I feel inadequate all the time.

T: Inadequate to do what? (*Shifts attention from label to process.*)

P: Well, it's not so much that I can't do things. It's really that I can't do anything without feeling that I'm not doing a good enough job.

T: Not doing a good enough job for whom? (*Shifts attention to missing references.*)

P: For other people.

T: Who is it specifically that you don't do a good enough job for? (*Shifts attention from generalization to concrete experience.*)

P: Well, mainly for my father. He's never satisfied with anything I do.

T: How well would you have to do something for your father to be satisfied? (*Shifts attention to unexamined possibilities.*)

P: He wants me to be the best at everything I do. When I'm in competition, it doesn't matter how well I do a thing. If someone else does it better, then he's not satisfied with my performance. (*Goes on to give examples of an essay contest and of a track meet.*) Obviously, my father doesn't love me.

T: To whom is it obvious? (*Rhetorical shift of patient's attention to the fact that all he is describing are his own conclusions about the interactions with his father.*) What you're saying is that your problem is that you feel inadequate all the time. It turns out that what you mean is that unless you win, your father's not satisfied with how well you perform in competitive situations. Because of that, you're sure that he doesn't love you, and the reason you give yourself for why he doesn't, is that you're an inadequate human being. (*Summary redefinition of the patient's problem in terms of the underlying structure elicited by the questions.*)

The therapist's careful use of structural questioning faciliates the patient's redefining of problems by becoming aware of their deeper structure. But this new awareness will not be lasting if mediated solely by this one intervention. The groundwork for its effectiveness requires that first the trust necessary to a therapeutic alliance be mediated by the intervention of reflection of feelings. The alliance will not by itself allow the patient the lasting expanded awareness that constitutes the Therapeutic Process. Within this, are needed the new experiences promoted by the confrontations of the character analysis.

If the combined work of these three interventions have been effectively carried out, the patient usually is free of original presenting complaints by the end of Phase I. Ironically, the successful completion of Phase I work may lead the patient to terminate at this point, having settled for relief from the original discomfort. The patient is unlikely to remain in treatment and to go on to Phase II without having become curious about the way he or she lives life, and interested in attaining a more intimate relationship with the therapist.

The first indication of completion of Phase I may come in the form of the patient's finding that there no longer seems to be much to talk about. This is often expressed in terms of having solved the problems that first led to seeking treatment.

As always, at this point I am quite willing to support the patient's wish to do as he or she pleases. But I am *not* willing to support the leaving in the absence of *understanding* the choice point that has been reached.

This has all the makings of a major impasse. Should I pressure him remaining in treatment, I will find that the staying/going conflict that resides within the patient will be divided into a tug-of-war *between us*. The patient is likely to insist that it is up to me to be convincing that it is worthwhile to spend more time and money in order to discover deeper problems and to endure more pain.

I communicate that I am quite willing to help in making this decision about the patient's life. I can be counted on to help in the leaving, *or* the staying, as the patient chooses. I can also be counted on to promote the patient's doing so as fully aware of what is going on inside as possible. Again I point out that *I do not care what he or she does.* I care only about fulfilling my commitment to continue to offer my expert service of heightening consciousness.

I go on to point out that the current misgivings about continuing to meet with me are very much like the doubts most people experience when they reach this threshold of the second stage of therapy. Making clear that I do not know whether or not it would be better to stay or to go, I invite further exploration of the matter.

With many patients, Phase II work requires that we meet more often. Focusing directly on the issue of increased frequency of appointments is one way I clarify and transcend the impasse that grows out of the patient's uncertainty about making the transition.

Having explored the patient's feelings about terminating the treatment at the end of Phase I, I sometimes offer a renegotiated contract at that point. I say to the patient: "It seems to me that you have gotten all that you can from this first stage of psychotherapy. It may be that you will decide that it is best for you to leave treatment now. Should you want to continue, it will be necessary for us to meet more often if I am to be able to fulfill my commitment of offering you my best work during the second phase. We can make today our last meeting. If instead you choose to go on, we will begin meeting twice a week," (or three times if we already have been meeting twice).

The patient may balk at my introducing this new parameter. In any case, we will need to discuss any feelings about it. I do *not* pressure the patient to stay on and to come more often. I do *not* explain further, nor do I try to convince that I am doing this simply for the patient's own good. Without caring whether he or she chooses to go or to stay, I concentrate on maintaining those conditions within which it is possible for me to do impeccable work.

Many patients respond with anger to my "arbitrariness." My interventions are aimed at promoting the patient's awareness of freedom and responsibility in deciding what he or she will do. It is up to the patient to choose whether or not to join me in this extended and deepening thrust toward self-discovery. Most of my patients *do* decide to go on, accepting our meeting more often as a meaningful development in their readiness to continue learning about themselves.

PHASE II

Other patients concentrate mainly on their sadness about our separating, and then they leave. Now that losing patients matters less to me, more patients stay on through the transition into Phase II. Should the patient continue into this second or middle phase of therapy, we are likely to spend one to three years of deepening intimacy. The patient will find that we get to know each other in new ways. He or she will learn a great deal more about the hidden self, and may resolve major underlying conflicts.

Throughout the entire course of the relationship, the therapist uses *silence* as the primary therapeutic intervention. During Phase II, its use is increased and extended. Silence is the most difficult intervention for a young therapist to learn to use effectively. Often, when quiet, the therapist's self-image may be that of someone who is "doing nothing." The patient in turn may feel that the therapist is withholding.

Early on in Phase I, I can let the patient know that I will only speak when I believe that I have something useful to say, and that I will never withhold anything that is likely to promote the Therapeutic Process. This explicit commitment can serve as a later frame of reference to support each partner's tolerance of the necessary silences.

The patient will often pressure the therapist to respond. It may not be an attempt to elicit some particular reaction, so much as seeking the reassurance of hearing the therapist's voice, or of feeling less helpless about being able to control his or her behavior. The therapist is also faced with internal pressures to speak. They arise out of the need to participate more actively, to be of help, to feel more effective, or to please the patient. Impatience with self will sometimes lead to breaking this silence in ways that are in opposition to the Therapeutic Process. In an attempt to offer something more useful than silence, the therapist may distract the patient from finding his or her own way in the pursuit of greater self-awareness.

Silence functions as a therapeutic intervention in a number of ways. For one, offering silence at those times when social expectations would demand conversational response, eliminates the deferential ceremonial gloss that serves to inhibit primitive impulses and fantasies in most social relationships. More broadly, it respects and encourages the patient's taking responsibility for setting the tone and directing the focus of the exploration. In an undemanding way, my silence simply makes room for the patient's unhampered attention to the internal flow of his or her own thoughts, feelings, and wishes.

During the silences, *the therapist is working!* Though silent, I am actively listening to the patient. To add to my understanding of what I hear, I recall the sequence that led up to this point. I note the relation of what is being said now to what the patient has told me at other times.

Linking the material in which the patient is presently immersed with what I already understand, I form silent hypotheses. If confirmed by the unfolding material, I may later offer these hypotheses as interpretations at times when anxiety and distracting defenses block the patient's flow of associations.

When the patient is pursuing self-exploration on his or her own, I remain silent. When I do not understand, I remain silent. Even if the patient, too, chooses to be silent, I may remain silent.

For most therapists, talking too much is the more common error. However, it is also possible for a therapist to be silent too long or too often. The most obvious problem in this is missing offering more active interventions when they are called for. Beyond that, excessive or overly prolonged silence may be an expression of counter-transference. That is, these silences may be ways of communicating unwarranted, anti-therapeutic attitudes arising as defense against the therapist's awareness of his or her own inner responses to being with a particular patient. At such times, silence communicates anger, contempt, or undue deprivation. It invites the impasse of a power struggle.

Even in the absence of the burden of the therapist's using silence to act out defenses, this intervention is open to all sorts of fantasied projections by the patient. It may be experienced as sadistic deliberate withholding, as disapproval, as uncaring passive sanction of the patient's wishes, as stubbornness, as an air of superiority, etc.

The therapist must come to understand the ways in which it is tempting to misuse silence. It is complicated enough to work with the patient's projected experience of these needed silences without the intricate underlay of the therapist unwittingly using them as a way of acting out unconscious conflicts.

During Phase II the effectiveness of the increased use of silence as a therapeutic intervention can be expanded and enriched by using the couch. When I speak of "using the couch," I am applying that phrase generically. In my own practice it refers mainly to giving the patient the opportunity to lie back in a reclining chair with eyes closed, curtains drawn, and office lights dimmed. Some patients prefer to lie on one of the courches in the office. Some choose instead to lie on the carpeted floor.

Either of these latter alternatives are acceptable to me. In either case, I explore the meaning of the patient's wish. Sometimes it turns out that a patient chooses to lie on the couch rather than to lean back in the reclining chair because the chair faces my chair while the position on the couch does not. This choice usually turns out to be a way of avoiding the symbolic vulnerability of lying back in a way that makes the patient feel sexually exposed to me.

I never insist that the patient use the reclining chair instead. Together we do explore the meaning of this sexual anxiety. Those patients who prefer to lie on the floor often turn out to be symbolically reliving early childhood experiences. Their fantasies usually include being children playing on the floor with a grown-up watching over them.

When the use of the couch is introduced to facilitate Phase II work, it is best done in response to the patient's reported difficulty in remembering dreams or early material, or in not knowing what to talk about.

At this point the therapist can respond by saying: "Perhaps I can help you with that. Many people find it useful in this phase of therapy to lie back in the chair with their eyes closed. It gives you an opportunity to be able to pay attention to what is going on inside without being distracted so much by my presence. Most people find that lying back in the chair (or using the couch) puts them in touch with forgotten memories, with dreams and fantasies, with neglected parts of themselves."

The patient will usually respond with some anxiety about being far away from me, fear of loss of control, or of support, etc. These anxieties must be explored and interpreted.

It is also necessary to attend to any fear that I am *making* the patient do this. One way to preempt this reaction is for me to discourage the patient's lying back before the uneasiness has been explored. This can be done simply by saying to the patient: "Why don't we put off your lying back until we understand better how you feel about it?" The patient usually will respond with relief and the necessary work can be undertaken.

When the patient's initial response to the introduction of the opportunity for use of the couch is completed, I may go on to say: "Should you want to use the couch to make it easier for you to get more in touch with yourself, from now on you will find the lights dimmed and the curtains drawn. My doing that does *not* require that you use the couch. I'll just be setting up the office so that you can lie back whenever you decide to begin that experience."

The patient may ask how long he or she is to use the couch. Is it to be one or two sessions, or from now on until the end of therapy? I may respond: "Most people find it useful to do this on a continuing basis over a period of time. Perhaps you could consider trying it for six months or a year and see how it works out." This suggested time period is always longer than what the patient really had in mind. It is not a demand, but it does open the imagination to the possibility of this being a long, continuing, useful experience.

Once having begun using the couch, there will be times when the patient will want to sit up with eyes open. I *neither give nor withhold permission*. It is up to the patient to choose how to use the therapy session. Like all other changes in the patient's behavior, I will note this. I may or may not choose to comment on it at that time.

The patient's sitting up is open to exploration and to interpretation. It may turn out to be a way of avoiding awareness of some inner experience, or it may be a way of facilitating an important encounter with me. It's very difficult for a person to express anger openly and effectively when lying back with eyes closed while the object of resentment is sitting up watching.

The Phase I work has established the trust needed for the therapeutic alliance, modified the character style enough to open the patient to new kinds of awareness, and redefined problems so that it is no longer necessary to have attention rooted to presenting symptoms. Commitment to go into Phase II turns the patient's attention toward further self-exploration. My increased silence promotes immersion in the Therapeutic Process. Use of the couch facilitates focusing on inner experiences.

As concentration turns inward, again and again the patient encounters the threshold of new understandings that are intensely upsetting. Consciously or unconsciously, self-protective defenses that have been learned in the past will re-emerge. At such times, I will offer the therapeutic intervention of *interpretation* as a way of restoring the patient's concentration on inner experience and flow of communications.

An interpretation is a statement by the therapist about the unconscious meaning of the patient's experiences or behaviors. If the formulation is correct and the timing is right, the interpretation will increase the patient's self-understanding by increasing awareness of unconscious fantasies and forgotten experiences.

Interpretations must be specific to the particular patient to whom they are being offered. General interpretations about what it is like for most people, about the relationship of anger to helplessness, about how shame affects behavior, etc., are educational in the intellectual sense, but do *not* further the patient's personal self-awareness.

If there is not enough information for me to formulate an interpretation at a point when one is called for, it is often useful to begin by simply calling attention to the sequence of productions. For example, a patient describes a series of events and then trails off into obsessing about the meaning of life. At that point, I might simply summarize what has been presented by saying, for instance: "Before you began philosophizing about life's meaning, you told me three stories of an unsatisfactory meeting with a woman. Each time you went off to hang around with the guys. Then you ended up in a fight." This pre-interpretive re-focusing often leads to unfolding of more related material.

A patient may present a long, complicated dream. I respond with silence. The patient tries to understand the dream but little or nothing comes to mind. This time I merely call the patient's attention to the manifest recurring motifs. In response to a particular dream I might point out: "Again and again in the dream, there is a surge of power followed by a disaster and then a restful calm." Like the re-focusing on sequence, this pointing up of recurring motifs often leads to enough new information from the patient to make the needed interpretation possible.

The practicing psychotherapist gradually develops a keener sense of the proper timing of interpretations. It is not enough for the content of an interpretation to be "correct." If the timing is not in phase with the patient's readiness to receive it, such an intervention will disrupt rather than promote the Therapeutic Process.

The most likely timing error occurs in the premature interpretation. I am *not* there to tell everything I know, but to offer that which is most likely to be useful to the patient at any given point. Premature interpretations confuse the patient, arouse undue anxiety, and evoke characteristic defenses against such distress.

Even if the patient accepts such a communication on an intellectual level, it will only provide a misleading foretaste that will make it harder later to reach an emotional understanding. Like an acid trip, at worst a premature interpretation is likely to be a bummer. At best it is a glimpse into heightened awareness that will not last.

The missed intervention of the interpretation that is withheld at a time when a patient is ready to receive it will also disrupt both the Therapeutic Process and the alliance. The patient will find ways to let the therapist know that he or she feels misunderstood. The interpretation must then be made late rather than never. Repair work to the relationship will need to be undertaken.

A child once instructed me about the patient's experience of the rightness of the timing of interpretations. I had been treating his mother and his father, both individually and as a couple. In some of their joint sessions, the parents had discussed their distress over their ten-year-old son's school difficulties. He had been diagnosed as a "hyper-active child." He was being treated by means of medicine and a behavior modification program with some success. The parents were concerned about their own emotional problems possibly contributing to the boy's difficulties.

There was no clear evidence of this, and there *was* a good deal of support for understanding the boy's problems as being physical in origin. Still I agreed to their bringing him to the office for an exploratory family session. He turned out to be a bright, highly verbal, somewhat physically over-active child. The medication he was taking allowed him to be calm enough to participate in our foursome discussion of what went on in the family.

By the end of the hour, it was clear to me and to his mother and father that he was receiving a good deal of wholesome parenting. His participation had helped all of us to understand more of what family life in his home was all about.

Before we ended the session, I asked him what the experience had been like for him. He answered: "I pretty much liked it, but you know, Shelly, you talk funny."

Intrigued by his comment, I asked him what he meant. His response was directed to the many interpretations I had made during the hour. He said: "Well, it's not just that you don't examine people and give shots like a regular doctor. It's more that lots of times when you tell me things about myself, they turn out to be things I know, but I don't know that I know them until you tell them to me."

Even when my timing is right, I must decide what sort of an interpretation to make. No interpretation is complete. Each is a fragment of understanding. At a particular time in the therapy, I may understand a good bit more about the patient's unconscious fantasies than the patient has as yet discovered.

My choice of interpretation first of all relates to what the patient is dealing with at the moment that the further unfolding of material is blocked. If I believe that I understand what might have made the patient so anxious as to distract attention from what was going on within, I may be able to offer an interpretation the content of which is "correct." However, no matter how "correct" the *content* of an interpretation, it will not promote the patient's reimmersion in the Therapeutic Process unless offered in a *form* that can be accepted by the patient.

An interpretation works best if it is brief, simple, and directly related to matters that the patient is consciously attending to at the time it is offered. It is stated in specific and personal terms that include the details of what is being discussed and the idiom in which the patient speaks.

My own spatial metaphor for the development of the patient's self-understanding is a spiral. In line with this, I order the sequence of the partial interpretations to be offered in a progression that gradually deepens understanding.

By going wherever the interpretations lead, the patient can go with the whirlpool current in which he or she is caught. The expansive consciousness will spin round and round past the same positions on the circumference of an ever-narrowing and deepening circle. At the bottom, the patient may finally arrive at the whirlpool's eye; that vortex from which he or she will spin free.

To facilitate immersion toward this vortex that is the culmination of the Therapeutic Process, my selection of the sequence of interpretations will be *from the rim to the center* and *from the surface to the depths.*

This next clinical example is offered as a way of illustrating some aspects of ordering the sequence of interpretations. In this fictionalized account of my work with a particular patient I will need to give more information than I have in previous examples. Though a bit more elaborate than the others, this description remains skeletal and intentionally trimmed in a manner that invites the reader's attention to the data that led to the interpretations in question.

The patient is a bright, competent, but rather shy young woman. She chose to enter therapy to try to overcome her restraint in revealing her inner self, hoping to learn to be able to get closer to people who matter to her. To judge from the apparent ease of this woman's overall creative functioning, it would be difficult to imagine the enormity of her burden of inner constraint and fearfulness.

Phase I work with this patient had fluidity and grace. Her adventuresomeness and keen intelligence made the joy and excitement of self-discovery a strong compensating balance for the pain evoked by some of what she had to face. Mediated by my concerned reflection of her feelings, a level of trust sufficient for the therapeutic alliance was soon established.

Character analytic confrontation made her aware of her stylized posture of living the life of a hidden saint. Having to be so specially caring and compassionate as she quietly went about saving the wretched of the earth, she often felt unappreciated by those who did not see her as beyond reproach. On the other had, her own perfectionistically high standards for herself led her to judge her realistic achievements as unworthy and her talented ways as those of a stumble-bum.

Structural questioning allowed her to redefine her problems by paying attention to the hidden context of her hyper-critical view of herself. She was able to see more clearly under what conditions she performed well, in what kinds of situations she had difficulties, and what her options for change might be. After a few months of Phase I transactions she had discovered that she did not have to work so hard or to make so many sacrifices for her life to be meaningful. She felt freer, more hopeful, and increasingly able to be closer to some of the people who mattered to her.

She was tempted to leave therapy at that time. We discussed this as a meaningful option. She decided to stay on, partly out of fear that she might miss more of the as yet undiscovered good things in herself. Partly she wanted to be a good girl by excelling as a psychotherapy patient. Her motivation also included her wish to be closer to me.

As we entered Phase II work, my extended silences, coupled with her fantasizing about lying back with her eyes closed, turned out to be more upsetting than she had anticipated. I discouraged her impulse to rush into the frightening experience of using the couch, supporting instead respecting her uneasiness and being kinder to herself by waiting until she felt more ready for the deeper explorations.

During this time she shared with me two recurrent fantasies with which she had been secretly obsessed for several years. The first she reported with embarrassment born of the demands of modesty and shyness. This fantasy involved her receiving international acclaim as an inspirational performer whose songs would teach the world how to live.

She felt ashamed as she described the violence of the second fantasy. It centered on an act of murderous vengeance against the authorities who brutally mistreat the helpless and the oppressed.

Soon after feeling safe enough to use the couch to turn the gaze of her closed eyes more deeply inward, she was intensely upset to find that what she faced was the void of her own emptiness. She *sensed* that she felt things deeply, but feared that she had no way of getting in touch with these feelings, or of ever being able to communicate to others what goes on inside of her. For a time she experienced only helplessness and despair. I offered silence, reflection, and redirection of her attention to what all this might mean to her. This led to her painful recognition of how deeply she felt that inside, she was really an awful person.

We both knew that there was more, but for a while she could not focus her inner vision. At times she spoke of being at the edge of almost remembering some hauntingly vague experiences. Slowly there arose in her consciousness, fragmented recollections of "ugly feelings" between her parents. Gradually she remembered their screaming at each other how awful the other one was. Accompanying these echoes of mother and father berating each other came the beginning of her re-experiencing her own small-child-terror at being exposed to these destructive arguments.

Suddenly her next association was the seemingly unrelated recollection that she had been "a great liar" at that age. When this was explored through structural questioning, it turned out that her harsh judgment about herself related to her remembering that as a small child she often lied to her parents. She told them tall tales of made-up accomplishments and fantasied awards for activities that had not really taken place. Her lying always involved some skill that she actually possessed, exaggerated by her creating some fantasy event in which she pretended it had been displayed. For example, she had been a strong athlete as a child, but would tell her parents about having won races that had never been run.

As she went on to berate herself for having lied to them, I realized that attention had been shifted away from her terrified description of her parents' battles. It was time to make an interpretation aimed at uncovering an unconscious fantasy, the avoidance of which was interfering with the Therapeutic Process of her expanding her consciousness of this aspect of herself.

I made several interpretations as the material developed over a number of sessions. Without attempting to recreate that dialogue, I will present the interpretations I offered in the order in which they were made.

Faced with the first option of interpreting the present or the past behavior, I began with *now*, only later going back to *then:*

PRESENT: "A little earlier this session you were talking about how terrible you felt when your parents fought and berated each

other. By concentrating now on how awful you feel about yourself
for lying to them, you have shifted your attention (and mine) away
from your feelings about Mother and Father."

PAST: "By telling your parents made-up stories about your
accomplishments, you were able to distract them from fighting
with each other."

Later the choice was between a surface and a deep content
interpretation. The order that best promotes the Therapeutic Process
is *from the top down:*

SURFACE: "You hoped that if only you could look good
enough to your parents, maybe they would be satisfied and stop
reproaching each other."

DEEP: "You believed that your parents were unhappy because
you were not a good enough child. If only you could fool them
into believing that you could accomplish whatever they might
want from you, then they wouldn't kill one another."

As my understanding was enriched by the patient's adding freshly-
freed elaborations of these earlier experiences, it was time to choose
the order of offering between the paired options of interpretation-
of-defense and interpretation-of-the-impulse against which the
defense had been established. The guideline is always to work
from the outside to the inside:

DEFENSE: "You wanted your parents to stop fighting because
you were afraid that they might hurt one another badly or separate,
and then there would be no one there to take care of you."

IMPULSE: "You tried to make them feel that you were so
special that they would ignore each other and only pay attention
to you."

The interpretation of transference, too, is made on *increasingly
deep levels.* First the unconscious fantasy-laden response to the
therapist is addressed. Later the focus is shifted to the original
object:

TRANSFERENCE: "Now that you are threatened with the temptation to leave therapy and can only stay by using the couch and having less contact with me, your old awful feelings about yourself come back. You are angry at me for seeming to put you in that spot, you exaggerate your prowess as a child-liar, warning me that you are so good at lying that I won't be able to make you feel vulnerable and helpless."

ORIGINAL OBJECT: "You told your parents how you used your power to accomplish wonderful things so that they wouldn't find out how much you hated them and wanted to destroy them for ignoring you and making you feel so awful."

A more complete interpretation would include all of these levels of understanding plus a comprehensive formulation of how this all arose, how it gets acted out in her adult life, and how it shapes her relationship with me. It would also focus on the meaning of those symptoms that first brought her into therapy (difficulty in getting close to people who matter because of her need to hide her feelings), on her character style (hidden saint who is beyond reproach), and on her obsessive fantasies (of messianic acclaim, and of vengeful terrorism).

An interpretation as complete as this is rare in therapy. Usually I do *not* understand enough to make one. The patient would be overwhelmed by such an intervention. In any case, the offering would require a mini-lecture that does not fit my role as the therapist.

Instead as I begin to understand, interpretive fragments are offered a piece at a time. Each selection is guided by the patient's apparent readiness to receive it. As the patient uses these communications to understand more and more of what goes on in his or her life, gradual combining and integration of these fragments occurs. Only in Phase III are more comprehensive interpretative summaries of use.

These criteria for the selection of interpretations are *not* unbreakable rules. They merely serve as guidelines. The fittingness of the interpretation for a particular patient at a particular point is a matter of exploration and discovery. Even an incorrect interpretation *may* be useful. It directs the patient's attention toward unconscious meanings and models as ways of thinking about them.

Often the patient can be counted on to correct the therapist's off-the-mark effort.

All of my Phase II interventions are aimed at deepening the patient's understanding of unconscious fantasies and feelings. Even correct interpretations will have to be repeated again and again in different contexts. In this way the meanings will be elaborated and enriched while the patient takes the needed time to integrate new understandings. It is a slow and gradual process.

The basic impasse during the second phase of therapy pivots on the patient's feelings of dependency and on the experienced helplessness to change. These, too, must be interpreted, but the patient cannot move beyond this stuck place until ready. No matter how expert my interpretations, people change at their own pace. Though no longer effective, their past ways of living have served them well up to a point. Changes may be worthwhile for the patient, but they bring with them costly losses of old familiar ways and frightening risks of new and untried experiments. I concentrate on heightening the patient's awareness, *not* on changing his or her life. One patient described the experience of going through Phase II of psychotherapy as "taking a Berlitz course in the language of the unconscious."

The basic spiralling sequence of the middle phase is the repeated again and and again:

> unfolding, regression and resistance, clarification and interpretation, further unfolding of new material, solidification of gain, regression-resistance, and so on.[19]

After a while, the patient's expanded awareness of the inner self is clearer and more available. The patient has come as far as it is possible to come at this point in life, with this particular therapist. The changed ways of living and attitudes are experienced as reliable and lasting. Without fully realizing it, the patient senses that the Therapeutic Process is approaching an end. It soon will be time to say goodbye.

This recognition does not come about simply or directly. Touching on both conscious and unconscious fantasies, as well as on painful earlier experiences, the anticipation of separation from the therapist evokes both anxiety and grief. Rather than surfacing directly, this growing awareness is usually implied in the expression of symbolic communications and defensive behaviors.

PHASE III

The transition from Phase II to Phase III (the termination phase) is ushered in by dreams, fantasies, and preoccupation with themes of death and dying, of birth and journeys, of loss and separation. I point up these recurring motifs and interpret them as the foreshadowing of the patient's entry into the final phase of therapy.

In response to this interpretation, (or at times preceding it) the patient may display one or more of the typical denials of readiness to leave. A flare-up of symptomatic complaints is common. Often, as if communicating the need to start over, the complaints are the return of exactly those that led to entry into therapy in the first place. Expressions of suddenly heightened dependency occur as the patient communicates feeling unable to manage without my help. There may be an unexpected appearance of "new" material that has a curiously hollow, made-up ring to it.

Often the unacceptable wish to separate is projected onto me. The patient complains that I am losing interest and want to get rid of him or her. Whatever the nature of the defensive denials, their interpretation must focus on the unspoken feelings that precipitated them. If I am indeed acting as if the patient is someone who does not seem to need therapy it must be pointed out that this is a response to the *patient's* seeming freer, less inhibited, and with more self-awareness.

The termination is *not* an abrupt dismissal of the patient. Phase III is *not* just a time for leaving, but an extended period for working through the conflicts and fantasies associated with separation. It may last anywhere from a few weeks to several months.

There will be *no decrease* in the number of times we meet each week. This phase is not a dilution or trailing off of our work together. It involves the patient's staying on, not simply to say goodbye, but to explore that aspect of self that relates to separation.

The ending was implied from the beginning when during the first session I talked to the patient about the usefulness of our not separating precipitously. The temporary interruptions of the Therapeutic Process occasioned by vacations and illnesses have already provided opportunity for preliminary preparation for the final separation we both must face someday.

In some instances, the termination may be arbitrary and premature. The patient or the therapist may leave the area, become incapacitated by physical illness, or grow irreparably dissatisfied with the misalliance. In such cases, the patient's *rage* will be the predominant reaction. When the termination is threatened by the satisfactory completion of a successful therapeutic alliance, the emphasis will be on *grief*. Even so, the rage must not be overlooked.

Disappointment is another dominant theme. The patient asks: "Is this all there is to it?" Something he or she had hoped to work out has not been accomplished. Or the fantasy of someday being completely happy and problem-free is at last seen as unrealizable.

Interpretations will be called for if it is to be understood that some of the hurt and disappointment is directed toward me. Part of that criticism will be grief over the final giving up of the hope for a perfect parent who would make all things wonderful. Part will be realistic recognition of my limitations and weaknesses. Every therapist's work with every patient is flawed. Both the patient and the therapist benefit when each recognizes these imperfections.

As in the first two phases, the work in Phase III is aimed at heightening the patient's self-awareness by promoting the Therapeutic Process. I retain my professional posture right through the last minute of the final session. Dropping the therapeutic posture is simply a way of acting out fantasies (both the patient's and my own). It also contaminates the alliance unfairly for the patient who might wish to return in the future for more therapeutic help.

In the main, the work of Phase III is restricted to concentration on the issue of separation, and to tying up loose ends of the conflicts that the patient has already explored substantially in the previous phase. The working through of residual material calls for my repeating, elaborating, and specifying the interpretations that first were formulated in Phase II. These completions afford the patient overviews that serve as ready frames of reference after therapy when new experiences call forth old and costly patterns of behavior. Equipped for further exploration by experience in the Therapeutic Process, the patient has the opportunity to continue the work on self-awareness for the rest of his or her life.

The separation work calls for *thematic interpretations*. Earlier expectation of the temporary interruptions necessitated by vacations focused the Therapeutic Process on the theme of separation. Now in a more intense and comprehensive way, the patient recognizes that the last phase of therapy has begun. Every association from then on relates to the final parting. *There is no way to change the subject.* Whatever materials come up can be dealt with in their own terms, but each transaction must also be interpreted thematically as part of the separation process.

These thematic interpretations are *not* offered as generalized comments on how human beings react to separation. Constrained only by the limits of my understanding, each thematic interpretation is related to this particular patient's life history, to his or her unconscious fantasies about separating, and personal ways of dealing with such losses.

As the patient moves toward fuller consciousness of what the imminence of the final parting means, the question of later contacts with me arises. I find that attempting a social-personal relationship between myself and ex-patients never really works. No transference is ever completely resolved. Attempts to have a new kind of meeting have all the limitations of a parent and a child attempting to "just be friends." The shadow of the therapeutic alliance haunts attempts to move beyond it. There is residual doubling of role not unlike the usually disastrous incestuous efforts to have a parallel relationship *during* long-term intensive psychotherapy.

Once the patient begins to accept that termination will *not* be followed by other non-therapeutic contacts, the question of returning later for more therapy may be raised. I can no more promise that I will choose to accept the patient's bid for an appointment in the future than the patient can promise that he or she will request such a contact. We both will have to wait and see. However, I can communicate that I am *not* now closed to the prospect of further work with the patient, if needed later on.

Some patients do return later to take up some phase of the process with which they were not yet ready to deal the first time around. More often a few months after termination a patient may call to ask for another appointment. If we should meet, most often it turns out to be around a new crisis in the patient's life, a bit of unfinished work on the relationship, or what one patient called "a visit to the grave." In any case, unless there seems sufficient reason to reopen an ongoing therapeutic alliance, it behooves me to restrict the contact to a single session. This is done by helping the patient to become aware of what he or she is struggling with, mediated by interpretations that emphasize the ordinariness of the distress, the patient's thrust toward independence, and focusing on the future rather than on the past.

Once having come to terms with the finality of the approaching termination, the patient will usually want to set a date for the last session. Most often this is linked to some external parameter such as the beginning of a vacation, the end of a month, or some symbolically significant anniversary. After analyzing the meaning of the choice, I find it most useful to point out to the patient that our original contract only calls for one session's notice. After a while the patient recognizes that it could be tempting to stay on forever, that it might be possible to continue to gain *something* from therapy for a long, long time, and that it is *not* going to get any easier to leave. The patient is then likely to come in one day saying: "Next time will be my last session." The romance of transference gives way to the realities of time, money, and energy that might be better spent.

It is not unusual for the patient to offer the fantasy of a parting gift, if not the actual gift itself. Its offering implies obligations not yet fulfilled. The acceptance of a farewell gift leaves some aspect of the finality of the separation undone. Any time that I have made the mistake of accepting such a token, I have regretted it later.

Sometime during what appears to be the last few sessions, I point out that neither of us will experience the full grief of our parting until *after* our last session. I always let the patient know what he or she means to me, but the work goes on right up to the end of the last session. With fifty minutes having passed, of this, our last time together, I simply say: "Our time is up. Goodbye."

End Notes

*Seami. *Works,* 14th Century Japanese manuscript, p. 54, quoted in *The Nō Plays of Japan,* by Arthur Waley, with letters by Oswald Sickert, Grove Press, New York, originally published in England in 1920, p. 46.

End-Notes for Chapter 1—West Meets East

1. Sheldon B. Kopp. *Guru* (1971), *If you Meet the Buddha on the Road, Kill Him!* (1972), *The Hanged Man* (1974), *No Hidden Meanings* (1975), and *This Side of Tragedy* (1977), all Science and Behavior Books, Inc., Palo Alto, California. *The Naked Therapist* (1976), EdITS Publishers, San Diego, California.
2. Judith Schmidt. *Psychotherapy as Paths of Being,* an unpublished doctoral dissertation, The California School of Professional Psychology, San Francisco, California, August 1975. My interview, pp. 271-289.

End-Notes for Chapter 2—The Yoke That Frees

1. Ernest Wood. *Seven Schools of Yoga: An Introduction,* A Quest Book, Published under a Grant from The Kern Foundation, The Theosophical Publishing House, Wheaton, Illinois, 1973, pp. 1-2. Date not given.
2. Patanjali. *How to Know God: The Yoga Aphorisms of Patanjali,* translated with a new commentary by Swami Prabhavananda and Christopher Isherwood, A Mentor Book, New American Library Inc., New Jersey, 1953, p. 126.
3. Daniel Noel (Ed.). *Seeing Castaneda: Reactions to the "Don Juan" Writings of Carlos Castaneda,* G. P. Putnam's Sons, New York, 1976, p. 59.
4. C. W. Nicol. *Moving Zen: Karate as a Way to Gentleness,* William Morrow & Company, Inc., New York, 1975, p. 93.
5. Baba Ram Dass. *The Only Dance There Is,* Anchor Books, Anchor Press/Doubleday, Garden City, New York, 1974, p. 6.
6. Ernest Wood. For a discussion of the full range of schools of Yoga.
7. Baba Ram Dass. P. 118.
8. Lawrence Le Shan. *How to Meditate: A Guide to Self-Discovery,* Bantam Books, New York, 1974, p. 55.
9. Quoted in Le Shan, p. 59.
10. Quoted in Patanjali, p. 57.

158

11. Le Shan. P. 54. (my italics)
12. Baba Ram Dass. P. 120.

End-Notes for Chapter 3—The Fundamental Requirement

1. Sheldon B. Kopp. *If you Meet the Buddha on the Road, Kill Him! The Pilgrimage of Psychotherapy Patients*, Science and Behavior Books, Inc., Palo Alto, California, 1972, pp. 111–113.
2. Harold C. Lyon, Jr. *It's Me and I'm Here! From West Point to Esalen: The Struggles of an Overachiever to Revitalize his Life Through the Human Potential Movement*, with a forward by Carl R. Rogers, Delacorte Press, New York, 1974, p. 156.

End-Notes for Chapter 4—Assuming the Posture

1. Mircea Eliade. *Patanjali and Yoga*, Translated by Charles Lam Markmann, Schocken Books, New York, 1975, p. 68.
2. Sheldon Kopp. *The Hanged Man: Psychotherapy and the Forces of Darkness*, Science and Behavior Books, Inc., Palo Alto, California, 1974, pp. 39–40.
3. Carl Whitaker. "Rules in Psychotherapy," an Unpublished Fragment (my italics).

End-Notes for Chapter 5—Beginnings and Endings

1. Lionel Tiger and Robin Fox. *The Imperial Animal*. Holt, Rinehart, and Winston, New York, 1971.
2. Sheldon Kopp. *The Hanged Man: Psychotherapy and the Forces of Darkness*, Science and Behavior Books, Inc., Palo Alto, California, 1974, p. 32.
3. Sheldon Kopp. "The Unceremonial Nature of Psychotherapy," *Journal of Contemporary Psychotherapy*, Vol. 5, No. 1, Winter 1972, p. 14.

End-Notes for Chapter 6—Changes

1. K. R. Eissler. "The Effect of the Structure of the Ego on Psychoanalytic Technique," *Journal of the American Psychoanalytic Association*, Vol. 1, No. 1, January 1953, pp. 104–143.

2. K. R. Eissler. P. 105.
3. Sheldon B. Kopp, Ph.D. *The Hanged Man: Psychotherapy and the Forces of Darkness.* Palo Alto, Ca.: Science and Behavior Books, Inc., 1974, p. 40.
4. Ernest Wood. *Yoga,* Penguin Books, Baltimore, Maryland, 1969, p. 220.

End-Notes for Chapter 7—Impasses

1. Jay Haley. *Strategies of Psychotherapy,* Grune and Stratton, Inc., New York, 1963, p. 10 (my italics).
2. Albert Ellis. "To Thine Own Therapeutic Lust Be True???: A Rational-Emotive Approach to Erotic Feelings in the Psychotherapy Relationship," A paper read in the Symposium, Erotic Feelings in the Psychotherapy Relationship—Origins, Influence and Resolutions, at the American Psychological Association Convention, August 31, 1963, Philadelphia, Pa., p. 3.
3. Albert Ellis. Pp. 6-7.
4. Leslie H. Farber. *The Ways of the Will: Essays Toward a Psychology and Psychopathology of Will,* Basic Books, Inc., New York, 1966, p. 109.
5. James Hillman. "The Feeling Function," in *Jung's Typology* by Marie-Louise von Franz and James Hillman, Spring Publications, New York, 1971, p. 82.
6. Edwin S. Shneidman and Norman L. Farberow. *Clues to Suicide,* Foreword by Karl A. Menninger, McGraw-Hill Book Co. Inc., New York, 1957. In addition to a great deal of useful information about suicide, this book contains a collection of genuine and simulated suicide notes. The reader can judge the paired notes and obtain a score reflecting the accuracy of his or her judgment with regard to genuine suicidal attempts versus suicidal gestures. Most readers find that by taking the test before reading the book, and then again afterward, they are able to improve their ability to make this discrimination.
7. Baba Ram Dass. *The Only Dance There Is,* Anchor Books, Anchor Press/Doubleday, Garden City, New York, 1974, p. 73.

End-Notes for Chapter 8—Phases and Basic Interventions

1. Lewis R. Wolberg. "The Handling of Resistance to Cure," *The Technique of Psychotherapy,* Grune and Stratton, New York, 1954, pp. 463-550.
2. Robert Langs. "Responses to Interventions," *The Technique of Psychoanalytic Psychotherapy,* Volume II, Jason Aronson, Inc., New York, 1973, pp. 31-139.

3. Robert Langs. *The Technique of Psychoanalytic Psychotherapy*, Volume I, Jason Aronson, Inc., New York, 1973, p. 279.
4. Sheldon B. Kopp. *The Hanged Man: Psychotherapy and the Forces of Darkness*, Science and Behavior Books, Inc., Palo Alto, California, 1974, p. 53.
5. Alexander Lowen, *Betrayal of the Body*, Macmillan, New York, 1967.
6. Rix Weaver. *The Old Wise Woman: A Study of Active Imagination*, G. P. Putnam's Sons (for the C. G. Jung Foundation for Analytical Psychology, Inc.), New York, 1973.
7. Frederick Perls. *Gestalt Therapy Verbatim*, compiled and edited by John O. Stevens, Real People Press, Lafayette, California, 1969.
8. Carl Rogers. *Client-Centered Therapy*, Houghton-Mifflin, Boston, 1951.
9. Sheldon B. Kopp. *Guru: Metaphors from a Psychotherapist*, Science and Behavior Books, Inc., Palo Alto, California, 1971, pp. 143-144.
10. Carl Rogers. *Mr. Vac*, A Tape Distributed by the American Academy of Psychotherapists. Tape Library, Philadelphia, Pennsylvania, 1960.
11. Carl Rogers.
12. Carl Rogers.
13. Wilhelm Reich. *Character-Analysis* (Third Edition), Orgone Institute Press, New York, 1949, p. 4.
14. David Shapiro. *Neurotic Styles*, Foreword by Robert P. Knight, The Austin Riggs Center Monograph Series No. 5, Basic Books, Inc., New York, 1965.
15. Lewis Yablonski. *Synanon: The Tunnel Back*, Penguin Books, Baltimore, Maryland, 1967, pp. 149-150.
16. I. H. Paul. *Letters to Simon: On the Conduct of Psychotherapy*, International Universities Press, New York, 1973, p. 52.
17. Richard Bandler and John Grinder. *The Structure of Magic: A Book About Language and Therapy*, Introductions by Virginia Satir and Gregory Bateson, Science and Behavior Books, Inc., Palo Alto, California, 1975.
18. Albert Ellis. *Reason and Emotion in Psychotherapy*, Lyle Stuart, New York, 1962. Ellis' major technique in psychotherapy is a kind of structural questioning aimed at making conscious and then altering hidden irrational premises.
19. Robert J. Langs. *The Technique of Psychoanalytic Psychotherapy*, Volume II, Jason Aronson, New York, 1974, p. 435.

Suggested Readings
on Basic Technique
in Individual Psychotherapy

Changes in Parameter

Ernst G. Beier. "Extratherapeutic Incidents," in *The Silent Language of Psychotherapy: Social Reinforcement of Unconscious Processes*, Aldine Publishing Company, Chicago, 1966, pp. 92–118.

K. R. Eissler. "The Effect of the Ego Structure on Psychoanalytic Technique," *Journal of the American Psychoanalytic Association*, Vol. 1, No. 1, January 1953, pp. 104–143.

Confrontation

Wilhelm Reich. *Character-Analysis* (Third Edition), Orgone Institute Press, New York, 1949, pp. 3–290.

Harry Stack Sullivan. *Clinical Studies in Psychiatry*, Edited by Helen Swick Perry, Mary Ladd Gawel, and Martha Gibbon, with a Foreword by Dexter M. Bullard, W. W. Norton & Company, Inc., New York, 1956.

Interpretation

Robert Langs. *The Technique of Psychoanalytic Psychotherapy, Volumes I and II*, Jason Aronson, Inc., New York, 1973.

Paradox

Jay Haley. *Strategies of Psychotherapy*, Grune and Stratton, Inc., New York, 1963.

Jay Haley. *Uncommon Therapy: The Psychiatric Techniques of Milton Erickson, M.D.*, W. W. Norton and Company, Inc., New York, 1973.

Reflection of Feelings

Carl R. Rogers. *Client-Centered Therapy: Its Current Practice Implications, and Theory,* Houghton Mifflin Company, Boston, 1951, pp. 3–231.

W. U. Snyder, et al. *Casebook of Non-Directive Counseling,* Houghton Mifflin, Boston, 1947.

Structural Questioning

Richard Bandler and John Grinder. *The Structure of Magic: A Book about Language and Therapy,* Introductions by Virginia Satir and Gregory Bateson, Science and Behavior Books, Inc., Palo Alto, California, 1975.

Albert Ellis. *Reason and Emotion in Psychotherapy,* Lyle Stuart, New York, 1962.

Index for Back To One